A YEAR OF QUESTIONS

how to slow down and fall in love with life

Fiona Robyn

*for Jason —
enjoy the journey.
Warmest,
Robyn*

Published by Lulu

A Year of questions: how to slow down and fall in love with life.
A Lulu book.

Published by lulu.com 2007
ISBN 978-1-84799-973-3

© Fiona Robyn 2006. All rights reserved.

A YEAR OF QUESTIONS
how to slow down and fall in love with life

For Steve, who's always there.

ACKNOWLEGEMENTS

I'd like to thank Alex Valy for making this book so beautiful, and Alison Hill for making sure it made sense. Thanks to Esther Morgan and Jacqui Lofthouse for keeping my muse healthy and happy, especially when she gets bruised. Thanks to Nicola Weller, Charlie Mounter, Susan Utting and Heather Butler for their careful reading and always-useful comments. Thanks to Jo Brogan for not being able to put my book down. Thanks to Fraser Dyer for, amongst other things, pointing me towards Lulu. Thanks to everyone who pointed out that one of the potential covers looked like a man about to commit suicide (not the look I was going for). Thanks to visitors to my Creative Living blog, and for all the support I've had from the world of blogs and bloggers. Thanks to all the people who appear in this book in various guises. And thanks to mum and dad and Duncan and Steve, of course. Most of all, I'd like to thank my readers. That means you.

*Have patience with everything unresolved
and try to love the questions themselves.*
Rainer Maria Rilke

If you engage in travel, you will arrive.
Ibn Arabi

CONTENTS

Introduction	10
How to use this book	14

Autumn: preparing for the journey

Taking care of yourself	18
Clearing space	28
Becoming curious	38
Moodling	48

Winter: getting lost and finding yourself

Inviting solitude	52
Staying with struggle	62
Searching for meaning	72
Moodling	82

Spring: changing direction

Redirecting energy	86
Taking risks	96
Commitment and resilience	106
Moodling	116

Summer: enjoying the ride

Engaging with life	120
Slowing down	130
Being here	140
Moodling	150

The end or the beginning?

Resources	156
The magic of Morning Pages	160
How to find a good therapist	162
Clearing space for creativity	162
Where next?	166
Further reading	167

INTRODUCTION

Who are you?
I wonder why you are holding this book in your hands. I wonder what you are hoping you might find here. I wonder about the journey that has brought you here. How many books you have read? How much advice you have listened to? How many times you have vowed to take more exercise and do more meditation and generally lead a wholesome, healthy and virtuous life? Are you ready for something different?

Who am I?
You might be wondering what qualifies me to be writing a book on falling in love with life.

I have my experience of being a curious person and learning about myself using whatever comes to hand – having honest conversations with friends, writing, listening to the blackbird singing in the garden, being in therapy, sitting still and doing nothing at all. I have my experience as a connoisseur of words – decades of soaking myself in poems, novels, letters from friends, books about artists and engineers and gardens and madness, until commas and speech marks were coming out of my ears. I also have my experience of being a therapist – hour upon hour of sitting in a small room with another person and trying to work out what the dickens it's all about.

But none of that will really make any difference to you. I'm a complete beginner at what might be helpful for you – how you can grow sweeter tomatoes, whether you want to learn Japanese or cake decorating, or why you feel so sad when an aeroplane flies overhead – because I don't know you yet.

I'm not offering easy answers to any of your difficult questions. I'm mostly offering you more questions. This book is chock-full of questions – both direct and implied. I hope that these questions will nudge you towards parts of yourself that you haven't seen in a while, and offer an opportunity for you to do something differently. I hope that such questions will help you to put your face right up close to life, so you can really drink in that golden honeysuckle scent, and relish the silkiness of the fur on your cat's belly.

Rather than advice, what I really hope to offer you is a space where you can start to hear yourself. You might think that your voice is whispering too quietly for you to hear it, or that it keeps leading you up the garden path. If so, you've not been listening long enough or closely enough. This book will help you to listen more carefully.

Oh – and I do love my life.

Choosing your travelling companions

Do you like to go on journeys alone or would you rather have someone sat next to you so you can complain to them about the heat and borrow their sun-hat?

If you travel through this book alone you'll enjoy the sights and bring some souvenirs home with you, but it might be a more memorable trip if you combine it with one or more of the following travelling companions:

Writing
Writing things down can help you to start unravelling the tangled ball of string clogging up that space between your ears. It can give you somewhere to record the marvellous moments (realising you've always wanted to be a dairy farmer) and the shitty ones (remembering your milk allergy). It can also be a place of your own to return to when things are getting tricky. See 'The magic of Morning Pages' in the Resources section for a good place to start.

A questions-buddy
Ask a curious friend to work through this book with you. Meet and discuss what comes up for each of you once a week or month.

A sketch pad, a lump of clay, a garden...
Whatever your favourite creative medium, make sure you give yourself enough space to play with it. See what comes up and whether your creative experience relates to any of the questions you've been asking yourself. See 'Clearing space for creativity' in the Resources section if you get stuck.

Meditation
Why is it so difficult to do nothing for fifteen minutes? Amongst other benefits, making a regular space in your day for meditation will help you to chew on your questions without getting indigestion.

Therapy
I've learnt more about myself in the therapy room than I have anywhere else. If you find a good therapist and stick with it for a while, therapy really does reach the parts that other self-development tools can't reach. See 'How to find a good therapist' in the Resources section for more information.

Are you ready?
Before you set off, a word of warning.

In my experience, this self-development lark can be a messy business. Feeling uncomfortable, frustrated, lost, pissed off, hopeless, ashamed or sad can be just a few of the occupational hazards. In fact, if you're feeling like this, then you can be sure that something useful is happening.

This is all very well, but if you're already a bit wobbly and you've got a dissertation to finish by next Wednesday, today might not be the best time to start reading this book. To really go into uncharted territory, we need to feel reasonably safe and secure where we are. The first section of the book is all about taking care of yourself, and if you get the wobbles later on you might want to revisit this section and find your feet again.

Bon voyage

We're all looking for something – a quick fix, a definitive answer, a way of avoiding pain and insecurity and responsibility and confusion and loneliness. We're all desperate at times for someone else to tell us what to do.

Are you unconvinced by people who promise to transform your life in three easy steps? Are you tired of running around from guru to guru? Are you ready to use this book as a mirror instead and begin to find the answers inside yourself? I'll be with you all the way. Let's go!

HOW TO USE THIS BOOK

This book is divided into four sections – Autumn, Winter, Spring and Summer. Autumn looks at preparing for the journey, Winter at how to get lost and find yourself, Spring at changing direction and Summer at enjoying the ride.

Each season is divided into three months, each beginning with a closer look at your questions for the month. For example, Autumn looks at how to take care of yourself, how to clear the space you need for the journey and how to prepare for looking inwards.

Each month has four musings. These are a little slice of my own or someone else's life and are designed to spark off some questions in you. At the end of each season you get a week off to catch your breath and mooch around the house – a 'moodling' week. As Brenda Ueland said in her book about how to write, '... the imagination needs moodling – long, inefficient, happy idling, dawdling and puttering.' I think we could all use a bit more moodling in our lives, whether we're artists or not.

If you are the super-organised kind of person who keeps your CDs in alphabetical order then you might like to begin at the beginning of this book and work through to the end. You can read the essay at the beginning of each month and then read a musing before breakfast every Monday. You could even be ultra-patient and wait until the leaves start to turn golden before you start.

If, on the other hand, your CDs are mostly out of their cases and sprinkled around the house and car, you might want to open the book at the section that most piques your curiosity. Have you been struggling with how to be alone? Try 'Inviting solitude'. What do you get when you let the book fall open and stick your finger on the page?

Or maybe you want to do the opposite of what you'd usually do, and see what that's like instead.

The words in this book are intended to be the beginning of something, and so there are plenty of resources and ideas about where to go next in the appendix.

Autumn

GETTING READY FOR THE JOURNEY

If the path before you is clear, you're probably on someone else's.
Joseph Campbell

TAKING CARE OF YOURSELF

If we want to move forwards with our lives, plunging into steamy rainforests or swimming through waterfalls, or groping our way through the dark, then we need to feel reasonably safe before we set off.

Now that we're grown-ups, we can't really rely on anyone else to keep us safe. We might not have been able to rely on anyone when we were children either, which makes learning to take care of ourselves especially important. Even those who love us most may do or say things with the best of intentions that are hurtful. If we don't recognise this pain and say 'no' or 'that hurt!' they'll probably keep on doing it.

Looking after ourselves is easier said than done. There are many reasons for this – feeling guilty about 'putting others out', not feeling worthy of kindness, and not knowing what we need amongst others. The first step towards getting better at self-care might be to think about why we're not already better at it. How was self-care seen by your family when you were growing up? What do you imagine people think about you when you do something for yourself? How do you see people who have good boundaries for themselves – do they intimidate you? Do you think they're mean?

The most important question is do we really want to look after ourselves? Way down in our murky depths, we all have traits, desires and feelings that we'd rather not know about. We do what we can to ignore them, but they have a nasty habit of popping up like mole-hills in the middle of a nicely mown lawn. How can we care about someone who enjoys gossiping so much? How can we want to be nice to someone who laughed when their sister fell over and hurt themselves?

The biggest challenge may be seeing ourselves for who we really are, including all the mean, greedy, arrogant bits, without wanting to cut those bits out and chuck them away. If we can acknowledge our spitefulness, and understand where it might be coming from, then we can start to make friends with it. We can start to make friends with ourselves.

The advantage of getting friendly with our messy bits is that we'll be more likely to accept other people with all of their messy bits too. Uncle Peter's reluctance to give away any of his tasty home-grown potatoes might make more sense if we've understood our own selfishness, and the fear of scarcity that sits behind it. It works the other way around as well – if we can be curious about why we despise Maria's ridiculously loud voice, we might discover that we're not too keen on our own desperation to be noticed either.

Perched on these foundations sit the skills and techniques that help us to look after ourselves. These include things like being able to say no, speaking assertively, making time for ourselves, doing more of the things we enjoy, and speaking to ourselves with an encouraging voice. Some people like to use positive affirmations or positive thinking and beliefs. If you do get stuck, however, be curious about what's going on under the surface. Are you using these techniques as a way of avoiding a nasty truth about yourself? What would happen if you got a little closer to the messy bit instead?

If you're out of practice at looking after yourself, you might want to ask yourself the same question over and over during the day until you drive yourself mad. 'What do I need right now?' It's not as easy as it sounds – we might answer that we need to have dinner with that handsome plasterer while our husband's away, or have a fourth slice of cake. How do we know that we're giving ourselves what is really good for us? Just keep asking. Deep down you know that it's not really good for you to escape from the problems in your relationship by hiding from them. You'll know that you'd rather go and get angry with that friend who disappointed you rather than stuff the anger down.

What do you need right now?

Week 1
MAYBE I'M NOT SO WEIRD AFTER ALL

This week a therapy client spoke to me about some of the things going on inside her head. Some of what she talked about was dark and ugly, and her face recoiled as the words came out of her mouth.

I listened as hard as I could, and I recognised the dark ugliness as something I had inside me as well, or something pretty similar. For a second, the shame of this flushed through me. My shame, her shame – same thing. I repeated back in my own words what I thought she was trying to describe to me.

We talked about what it was like for her to hear herself 'reflected in me' like this. She was amazed that it was possible for me to understand what she was saying, to make sense of it. And if I could understand what it is like to be her, then maybe the dark things inside her weren't as impossibly terrible as she thought. Maybe neither of us was so weird after all.

It's not always that simple – sharing is always a risk. My client was taking a huge risk – maybe I wouldn't understand her and she'd be left feeling more isolated than ever, or maybe I'd find her darkness too much and reject her. We have to be careful about who we choose to reveal ourselves to. But sometimes it's a risk worth taking.

Things you might be curious about

How much do you seek to be understood? How good are you at seeking to understand? When was the last time you really listened?

Suggestions for this week

Take a risk to speak and be understood. Take a risk to understand what someone else is really saying.

She did not talk to people as if they were strange hard shells she had to crack open to get inside. She talked as if she were already in the shell. In their very shell.
Marita Bonner

I loathe the expression "What makes him tick". It is the American mind, looking for simple and singular solutions, that uses the foolish expression. A person not only ticks, he also chimes and strikes the hour, falls and breaks and has to be put together again, and sometimes stops like an electric clock in a thunderstorm...
James Thurber

Week 2
CONVERSATIONS WITH YOUR BODY

Once a month I see an aromatherapist who sorts out the knots in my shoulders. She always starts our sessions by letting me know how stressed I've been since we last met – she's always right. Then she stirs together a delicious smelling concoction of oils, pushes her finger tips and palms into my flesh, and the tension-knots sigh, let go of themselves and melt away.

This week we had a conversation about the links between bodies and emotions from our different perspectives. Her clients often report feeling emotional for a day or so after they see her, after deep-down tension is 'brought out' and 'released' into the body.

This can be explained rationally by the way the body holds on to tension – we've all had a stress headache or felt physically tired after an emotionally difficult day. Bigger events also leave a mark on our bodies, but sometimes the marks live deeper down or are locked away.

I was telling my aromatherapist about how my therapy clients often report changes in their bodies after 'letting go of' or 'getting in touch with' bundles of emotion – they feel physically 'lighter', or 'more grounded'.

I had a conversation with my body this week. I'm not exactly sure what it's telling me yet but I feel a bit more in touch with myself, a bit less 'spacey'. I'm going to carry on listening and hopefully things will become clearer. At least we're talking!

Things you might be curious about

What does your body 'do' when you feel stressed/angry/sad? How 'in touch' with your body are you? Is it trying to tell you something?

Suggestions for this week

Twice a day, tune in to your body and notice how it feels. Where does it feel tense? Relaxed? What is your posture like? Are there any nagging aches? Does it feel tired, sad, worried? If your aches could speak, what would they say? Give your body whatever it needs – a stretch, a straighter back, a hug.

The body says what words cannot.
Martha Graham

It's also helpful to realize that this very body that we have, that's sitting right here right now... with its aches and it pleasures... is exactly what we need to be fully human, fully awake, fully alive.
Pema Chodron

Week 3

HOW TO FEEL MISERABLE AS AN ARTIST

I've been reading Keri Smith's blog, Wish Jar Journal, (www.kerismith.com/blog) for some time. I love her bright sparky colours, her quirky sense of humour, her wise and encouraging words.

I think most of all I admire her ability to share her vulnerabilities without diminishing herself or her credibility and power as an artist and as a person – no mean feat.

This week I'd like to share one of her lists with you (below, with her permission). Amongst other things it's about how easy it is for us to discourage ourselves, to beat ourselves over the head, by listening to what other people think about who we should be. If you're not an artist substitute 'father' or 'telephone engineer' or simply 'human being'.

How to feel miserable as an artist (or, what not to do – underline any that currently apply):

1. Constantly compare yourself to other artists.
2. Talk to your family about what you do and expect them to cheer you on.
3. Base the success of your entire career on one project.
4. Stick with what you know.
5. Undervalue your expertise.
6. Let money dictate what you do.
7. Bow to societal pressures.
8. Only do work that your family would love.
9. Do whatever the client/customer/gallery owner/patron/investor asks.
10. Set unachievable/overwhelming goals to be accomplished by tomorrow.

Things you might be curious about

What have you underlined? How does this affect how you feel about yourself? How could you begin to listen to yourself, encourage yourself, look after yourself better?

Suggestions for this week

Pick one of the following: hold all the advice you're given at arm's length and decide whether you'd like to listen to it or not, do something your family or friends would disapprove of (as long as it's legal!), cheer yourself on, become aware of the voice that criticises you inside your head and give it a different script, do something you want to do but won't get paid for.

The individual has always had to struggle to keep from being overwhelmed by the tribe. If you try it, you will be lonely often, and sometimes frightened. But no price is too high to pay for the privilege of owning yourself.
Friedrich Nietzsche

Anything you fully do is an alone journey.
Natalie Goldberg

Week 4
GIVING FROM A PLACE OF PLENTY

I sat down to write this musing yesterday morning but I felt reluctant, resentful; I wanted to be out walking in the September sun. I could have forced myself to sit down and plough through it, but I would have been giving from an empty place.

Giving from an empty place can often pay off in the short term. A friend asks to borrow some money, and we don't really have much spare but we say yes. Our partner asks us for a lift somewhere – we've just settled down on the sofa with a book but we put it aside and put on a smile. Everyone's happy.

But over time giving from a place of empty costs us and those around us. Giving from this place can use up a lot more of our energy than giving when we want to give. And all the little resentments that we think we're covering up can slip out in unexpected ways.

Often we just need to grit our teeth and get on with it – saying, 'I don't really feel like feeding you tonight' to a hungry three-year-old isn't an option. But maybe it is possible to look after our 'giving reserves' a little more carefully – by saying no when we need to, by giving more to ourselves. In the long run we'll probably end up giving more, and what we give will be given gladly and with love.

Things you might be curious about

How often do you give from an empty place? From a place of plenty? How does it feel different? How can you start to fill up your giving reserves?

Suggestions for this week

Give yourself something every day this week – a cup of cocoa with cream on top, half an hour longer in a lavender bath, a ride on your motorbike, a bunch of tulips. At the end of the week, choose something to give to someone else – a hand-made card, a shoulder massage, breakfast in bed. Choose something that you genuinely want to give.

Rich gifts wax poor when givers prove unkind.
William Shakespeare

Blessed are the generous who keep enough for themselves so we can live with them without guilt. Blessed, too, are those who receive well, so the generous get their reward.
Stephen Dunn

CLEARING SPACE

If we're serious about being curious, then we need a little space to be curious in. It's not easy to muster up a desire to question the meaning of life if we've got six loads of washing to do and twelve letters to write and four people to phone and a flat-pack cupboard to finish before it's time for tea.

Most of us are pretty clever at filling up our spare space. We can use all kinds of nifty tricks. We might pretend that it's necessary to do a 13-hour day to keep our job, when really we could look for a different job or just tell our boss that we're not doing it any more. We might put everyone else's needs before our own and feel smug about helping them when we're really just preventing them from finding their own solutions (and avoiding our own problems into the bargain). We might be convinced that the whole system would fall apart if we stopped to have a rest.

The trouble with making space is that it might mean you do have to go somewhere unpleasant. You might realise that you really don't like your job, or that you feel lonely. You might have to admit that you haven't a clue about what you're doing. This is the most common reason for keeping our lives nicely filled up. We don't want to risk falling down into the gap.

Falling into the gap and hurting our ankle a bit is better than getting to the finish line and realising that we've been running the wrong race. Falling into the gap gives us an opportunity to look again at what we're doing, at where we're going, at who we are. It gives us a chance to catch our breath. It might even be nice down there in the gap. You might enjoy watching the clouds and then the stars, forced to rest for a while, flat on your back.

It might help us in our quest for space to think about death. I know – it's not usually a popular subject in self-development books – but if you remembered that you might die in three years or three months' time, would you really be so keen to sort your socks into colour-coded drawers rather than go out and buy daffodil bulbs? Would you really rather moan to a drinking buddy about your partner than go home and have a proper conversation with them? Would you prefer to tidy the garden shed or sit and watch butterflies suck sweetness from the Buddliea?

I'm not saying that the garden shed doesn't need tidying. We all have responsibilities – children to look after, money to earn, potatoes to peel and drains to unblock. The trick is to find a way to get all this done and still find time to play. As the film character Ferris Bueller once said, "Life moves pretty fast. If you don't stop and look around once in a while, you could miss it." He knew what he was talking about.

Our lives so easily become clogged. Clothes that don't suit us clogging our wardrobe, unimportant worries clogging our minds, people we don't want to spend time with clogging our diaries. Someone else might appreciate that shirt with pink, orange and green stripes – give it away! Your ex-colleague Sue has a sneaking suspicion that you're not really interested in her holiday anecdotes – tell her, or meet up with someone else instead!

Clear a space. Clear some time, some energy, some physical space, some mental space. Clear a space, and keep it clear. Wait. Don't fill it back up – however uncomfortable it gets. Just wait. Feel yourself teeter a little. Then wait a little more.

Week 5
SIMPLICITY

Today I travelled back from Scotland and stopped off at one of those horrible motorway complexes full of burgers and artificial light and over-priced, plastic-wrapped, chemical-laden food. In the middle of all of that I found a smoothie that contained:

1/2 crushed mango
1 crushed passion fruit
1/2 crushed banana
2 pressed apples
1 freshly squeezed orange

Just fruit. It was delicious.

It fitted in nicely with all the reading I've been doing recently about the 'voluntary simplicity' movement. Voluntary simplicity is all about becoming conscious of what's unnecessary. It encourages us to get rid of the clutter in our lives – stuff, relationships, commitments – and to truly appreciate what's left. An inevitable consequence of simplifying seems to be a greater awareness of our responsibilities to ourselves, to each other and to the planet.

We don't have to sell all our possessions and go and live in the woods to join this movement. It's about choosing to recycle our Christmas tree, or saying no to that 14th pair of shoes. It's about being clear about what's important to us so we can channel our energies into the right places. Simplicity can even be found in a roadside service station.

Things you might be curious about

What parts of your life are overly complicated? What responsibilities do you currently have that are distracting you from where you want to be heading? How much of your money/energy do you funnel channel into consuming 'stuff' that doesn't quite give you what you're looking for?

Suggestions for this week

Choose one area of your life to de-clutter this week. This might be your bookshelves (give the books you don't want away to friends), your diary (what commitments do you want to say no to?), or your finances (do you really need to spend £6 a day on take-away coffee?). Make a list of other areas of your life that could do with some simplifying and tackle them one at a time over the coming weeks and months.

I am beginning to learn that it is the sweet, simple things of life which are the real ones after all.
Laura Ingalls Wilder

The ability to simplify means to eliminate the unnecessary so that the necessary may speak.
Hans Hoffman

Week 6
THE SOUND OF SILENCE

This weekend I'm off to Salisbury for a day-long meditation. There will be an opportunity to sit still in a silent room with other people for half-hour intervals from 10 am until 3 pm. Nobody will look into each other's eyes once we have begun. We'll be on our own.

There's a part of me that can't wait for this. A whole day to sit and just be. And there's another part that's terrified! What will it be like to stop 'doing' for so long? What will emerge from the silence?

This meditation day is a chapter in my ongoing battle between clearing space in my life and filling it back up again. No sooner have I arranged a free weekend or cut back on a commitment, than I find myself saying yes to something else, or deciding to start a new writing project.

I know that more space is a good thing for me. It feeds my muse, and it puts me back in touch with who I am and what I really want. But I need to acknowledge that it's scary too. Sometimes it's only when we give ourselves enough space that we get ill, or feel sad or angry. What have I been trying to avoid?

Things you might be curious about

What happens when you give yourself enough space to get in touch with yourself? What resistance do you have to doing nothing and just being? What opportunities might you have to stop doing and start being a bit more?

Suggestions for this week

Put aside a short period of time each day to be quiet, or a longer period at the weekend. Sit and do nothing. During this time, note the thoughts and feelings that arise and then let them go. Afterwards, be gently curious about what came up for you.

I love the deep quiet in which I live and grow against the world and harvest what they cannot take from me by fire or sword.
Johann Wolfgang von Goethe

If one is out of touch with oneself, then one cannot touch others.
Anne Morrow Lindbergh

Week 7
LESS IS MORE

After an expensive shopping trip today I had a flash-back to early last December. I had to queue up for a parking space, and the streets were seething with people in a frenzy of consumerism. There were hundreds of them wandering about with twelve different plastic bags each, bulging (I imagine) with novelty boxer shorts and chocolate Santas and fancily packaged letter openers and millions of other things that we don't really need.

It's not that I'm anti presents – any tradition that encourages us to appreciate the people we love has got to be a good thing. But I do wonder if anyone is any happier now that we buy more? Do the 105 extra minutes we get on the limited edition DVD really add anything to the film? Have we forgotten how to do anything without getting out our wallets?

Things you might be curious about

Where could less be more in your life? How does having more make you feel? More secure? Less unhappy? More successful? Do these feelings last? What might happen if you got in touch with what's underneath instead?

Suggestions for this week

Choose one area of your life where less will be more. Take some action. Suggestions are: not buying a new book but re-reading one you already love, cutting down on the time you spend with acquaintances and spending more time with your close friends and family instead, reducing your working hours and expenditure and enjoying your extra free time.

Perfection is finally attained not when there is no longer anything to add but when there is no longer anything to take away, when a body has been stripped down to its nakedness.
Antoine de Saint-Exupery

Our life is frittered away by detail. Simplify, simplify.
Henry David Thoreau

Week 8
A WINDOW, A SPACE

This week, work has been very stressful. Today I made soup.

I gathered the vegetables together in the kitchen – ordinary vegetables – carrots, potatoes, onions, leeks. I rubbed dark crumbly earth from the potatoes with my fingers. I fried the onions, releasing clouds of their caramel aroma into the room. I sliced the squeaky leeks. I noticed the brilliant orange of the carrots. I boiled the water and listened to it plobbing and ribupping.

As I moved around the kitchen I felt a kind of release. I reflected on my work, and untangled some knots. I made a couple of little decisions that will make a big difference. I said some kind words to myself.

I often return to this creative space, whether I'm making soup or cards or novels. It gives me an opportunity to become absorbed in an attempt at beauty. It gives me a chance to step out of being 'someone in relation to someone else' – a partner, a daughter, a therapist. I get to be me, pure and simple.

Things you might be curious about

How often do you give yourself the space to keep track of yourself? How committed are you to making this space? What gets in the way?

Suggestions for this week

Make a date with yourself this week to find out about a new creative pursuit or revisit an old one. Find an evening class in welding, buy a new sketch-pad, make a collage of the inside of a spaceship with your children, collect leaves in the park, get a Greek recipe book out of the library.

We all need to have a creative outlet – a window, a space – so we don't lose track of ourselves.
Norman Fischer

When we let ourselves respond to poetry, to music, to pictures, we are clearing a space where new stories can root, in effect we are clearing a space for new stories about ourselves.
Jeanette Winterson

BECOMING CURIOUS

When I think about curiosity, I think about a path winding through a higgledy-piggledy cottage garden and ducking out of sight around a tall hedge. I think about someone setting a never-tasted dish of rasmalai in front of me, and saffron, cardamom and rose scenting the air. I think about reading a sentence on the back of a book that speaks directly to me about a problem I've been caught up in for months.

For me, curiosity is an energy that pulls me out of my seat and gives me a direction. It tells me that I'm intrigued by forging, and that I should have a character who works in a forge in my next novel. It tugs on my skirt when I'm walking through a new city, and leads me down a narrow alley-way to where I find the necklace I've been searching for. It asks me to pause before I snap at my colleague, and think about what got me so ruffled. It points me towards the thing that I need to learn next.

Curiosity doesn't always speak to us directly about where it's leading us. I might not know why salsa dancing appeals to me, but if I give myself a chance I'm bound to find out. It might be that I need to feel my body shimmying and gyrating, or simply that I want somewhere to wear my green flouncy dress. Maybe my curiosity was going on a hunch that turned out wrong and I'll hate it – maybe ballet will be the thing. Our curiosity is working in the dark and it may take us a while to feel our way forwards, tripping over the cat and bumping into the corner of the table as we go.

Sometimes curiosity is really telling us where not to go. If we can't stop flicking through the job adverts, our curiosity might be suggesting that we start to work on the problems we're having with our critical boss. Curiosity isn't an excuse to take the easy way out. If we feel a nagging desire, it doesn't mean we should always obey it, but it will certainly be telling us about something in our lives that needs our attention.

When we're young, we're curious about everything. We want to know how aeroplanes work, why the sky is blue, and why Aunty Marjory is wearing that silly hat. We don't want to know how aeroplanes work so we can design new wings and sell the plans for lots of money, but because we wonder at how something so heavy and solid can float through the air like a dandelion seed. We love new knowledge for its own sake, and we gulp it down like iced lemonade on a hot day.

As we grow up our curiosity begins to lose strength. It might be told 'no' too many times by other people or ourselves – disapproved of, or discounted. We might feel we don't have any time to be curious – we're too busy keeping our heads above water with the busy job, the demanding father-in-law, and the nagging doubts. We might simply get out of the curiosity habit.

We can coax it back. We can become more conscious of our fledgling curious feelings, and capture them in a journal or share them with a friend. We can reward these little flashes of curiosity by following our noses and finding things out – asking someone who knows, searching the web, going on a day trip. We can create more space in our lives to let curiosity in. Curiosity is sitting inside you like a child indoors on a summer's day, just waiting to be asked by the boy next door to come out and play in his paddling pool. It won't need much encouragement.

Without curiosity, we would wear a narrow dirt path into our lawns as we walked from the back door to the washing line. We wouldn't wander over to get a closer look at that amaryllis, and find that bright green frog hiding in the bushes. Curiosity smiles a mysterious smile and beckons us forwards. It helps us to find out what we enjoy doing, what we want to know more about, and how we might do things differently. It helps us to find out who we are.

Week 9

WHAT'S GOING ON BEHIND THE CUP OF TEA?

I do some work as a telephone counsellor, and we get calls from people looking for some support when they're in crisis.

Sometimes when people explain the situation they're in, it's difficult to understand why they're so upset. It can be difficult to be sympathetic. This morning I spoke to a woman in floods of tears. Her main complaint was that she couldn't easily get a cup of tea at work on Wednesdays.

Later I spoke to another man who told me he was losing sleep and finding it difficult to eat. He was desperate to leave his job and couldn't stop thinking about what had happened. This reaction was to a single, off-hand comment from a colleague, who'd compared his work unfavourably with another colleague's. He couldn't understand why it had affected him so severely, and neither could I.

As our conversation went on a memory arose about the way his father always compared him (unfavourably) with his older brother. Bingo. He wasn't just upset by his colleague, but by an old family 'wound' that still stung like billy-o.

I didn't get very far with the woman who couldn't get a cup of tea – I didn't listen carefully enough, or she wasn't ready to tell herself what was really wrong. I do know that she really was hurting. Whether we unravel the meaning or not, there is always something behind the cup of tea.

Things you might be curious about

What are your 'cups of tea'? When have you had a stronger reaction to something than you would expect? What did the situation remind you of? What is the first childhood memory that comes to your mind?

Suggestions for this week

Whenever you notice someone's reactions this week, try to pause before you form a judgement (how pathetic/how arrogant/how selfish/how mean). Try to imagine what reasons they might have for acting this way. If it feels appropriate, ask them why they think they feel so upset/angry/hopeless. Listen carefully.

Every day, every day I hear
enough to fill
a year of nights with wondering.
Denise Levertov

Life has its own hidden forces which you can only discover by living.
Soren Kierkegaard

Week 10
THE MATING HABITS OF CENTIPEDES

I've always admired people who are passionate about something. Their enthusiasm fizzes over whenever they talk about their subject. It might be model trains, or the mating habits of centipedes, or making perfect ice-cream – it doesn't matter what. If you spend too long in their company you become in danger of catching it yourself.

Where do these passions spring from? I'm moving slowly but surely towards being passionate about growing things at the moment, and I'm asking that question of myself.

There's something about gardening and nature that has always appealed to me, but I've never been this excited by tulip bulbs before. It's only since I started immersing myself in the world of gardening for my second novel that my interest has started slowly blossoming into a passion. Reading about lilies, meeting lifelong gardeners, growing my own basil on the kitchen windowsill, building a collection of brilliant blue pots on the patio...

I'm happy to welcome a new passion into my life – it's already given me wheel-barrowfuls of pleasure. Maybe I'll even become infectious, serving my home-grown potatoes when people come for dinner and thrusting sweet-pea and strawberry seedlings upon strangers. All my passion needed was the right soil.

Things you might be curious about

What interest do you have that could be cultivated into a passion if you gave it enough attention? Who do you know who already has a passion? Could you open yourself up to basking in the glow of their enthusiasm?

Suggestions for this week

Create some regular space for a curiosity you already have – by booking yourself onto a course on Chinese pottery, buying a new box of tools to work on your scooter, or asking a friend to teach you how to ballroom dance.

Develop interest in life as you see it; in people, things, literature, music – the world is so rich, simply throbbing with rich treasures, beautiful souls and interesting people. Forget yourself.
Henry Miller

Only passions, great passions, can elevate the soul to great things.
Denis Diderot

Week 11
WHAT TO DO IF YOUR GLASSES ARE SMUDGY

Last week I had a conversation with a man I hadn't met before, and half-way through he mentioned his 'partner'. Just before I opened my mouth to ask a question, I caught myself assuming that his partner was a 'she' – a piece of information I hadn't actually been given. This assumption was proved wrong later in the conversation.

If it wasn't for some training I'd attended the weekend before about working with people from sexual minorities, I wouldn't have caught this slippery-fish automatic thought, even though I have made the same wrong assumption several times previously in my life. This assumption has been popping up so automatically that it hasn't even been available for discussion.

The experience reminded me of the phenomenological (go on, say it out loud!) technique of bracketing. Bracketing is where we attempt to leave our previous experiences and opinions 'outside the room', as if taking off a pair of smudgy glasses. If we are offering a guest a cup of tea, we 'bracket' our previous experience that everyone takes milk. If we are looking at a piece of cheese in the supermarket, we 'bracket' the assumption that supermarket cheese is fresh, and look more closely to see the spots of mould.

How much space are we leaving to be curious if we've decided so much about something before we've even looked at it properly? How likely are we to hear our next door neighbour's stories about their time as a tight-rope walker if 'all old people are boring'? How likely are we to try to sketch if we 'can't draw'?

Take off your smudgy glasses. Snuggle right up to new situations, objects and conversations and experience them as they really are.

Things you might be curious about

What assumptions are you aware of making about people/places/situations? How might these assumptions make your experience of life less rich?

Suggestions for this week

Try to root out some of your hidden assumptions. Suggestions are: when you express an opinion on something, imagine why someone might feel the opposite. When someone corrects you in a conversation, be aware of what assumption you've made. Ask your friends when you're particularly 'blinkered'. Listen very carefully to what other people say and check with them that you're hearing them correctly.

Assumptions are the termites of relationships.
Henry Winkler

The sceptical tradition that I draw upon is concerned with constantly questioning and self-questioning what we do know – or think we know – and how we come to know it, not in order to 'deconstruct' knowledge (whatever that might mean) but in the pursuit of truth.
Paul Gordon

Week 12

A SUMMER FRUIT SMOOTHIE

I spent yesterday in a fuggy too-warm office, and all day long I'd been looking forward to blending up a smoothie with cool orange juice and frozen summer fruits and sweet banana.

I hadn't used the smoothie-maker for a while, and when all the ingredients were added to the jug I pressed the 'whizzing' button and nothing happened. I fiddled with it for ten minutes, I tried a different plug... no whizzing. The lumps of frozen strawberry just stared up at me from the jug, smugly.

After several minutes of wallowing in a fog of disappointment and 'it's not FAIR!'-ness, I stopped for long enough to look around the kitchen. I spotted my hand-held soup-whizzer, right there on the shelf. Three minutes later I'd transferred the smoothie ingredients into a bowl and whipped them up.

The smoothie was as cool and smooth and sweet as swimming in the sea. After each sip the purple liquid clung to the inside of the glass as it flowed back down. It held onto hundreds of tiny air bubbles which let the light through in fierce pin-pricks. Mmmm...

Things you might be curious about

Are you holding on too tightly to any disappointments? How are they affecting your creativity, your ability to make choices and move forward? If you decide to let go, what could you have or do instead?

Suggestions for this week

This week, become aware of any small disappointments or annoyances. After allowing yourself to feel sad, let go of them and look around you. See what happens.

Creativity can solve almost any problem. The creative act, the defeat of habit by originality, overcomes everything.
George Lois

No man with a man's heart in him, gets far on his way without some bitter, soul searching disappointment. Happy he who is brave enough to push on another stage of the journey, and rest where there are living springs of water, and three score and ten palms.
John Mason Brown

Moodling

Week 13
GIVING THE SERGEANT MAJOR A WEEK OFF

I am a pretty disciplined person when it comes to my writing. There are probably lots of reasons for this but the main one is that if I wasn't, it wouldn't get done. Real life is far too rude, butting in with stupid questions, demanding my attention, tugging on my skirt and pulling me away from my writing desk.

Sometimes I let the sergeant major in me get carried away. I sit myself down and make myself write 1000 words when I actually need something different.

This week I have managed to listen to myself and instead of working on my novel, I'm working on something more important. I need a bit more space for this – a bit more time than usual to stare out of the window or potter about planting crocus bulbs in the garden.

The scary bit is trusting that I'll be able to sit down at my desk again next week, or next fortnight, when I'm ready. The scary bit is trusting that it really is better for me to have some swishy time this week, rather than it just being a more sophisticated excuse than usual to put off writing.

Who knows? But maybe we could all do with a break from whatever we're doing every so often, just to see what might happen.

Things you might be curious about

In what areas of your life are you highly disciplined? (I'm sure there must be one!) What would it be like to give yourself a break?

Suggestions for this week

Write a few pages about your experience of reading this book so far. What has been niggling you? What feels uncomfortable? What have you been putting off? Put these pages away somewhere and give yourself at least a week to enjoy doing something different – seeing friends, watching TV, going water-skiing. Have another look at what you've written when you feel the urge and decide what you'd like to 'pick up' again.

"Do you consider yourself a disciplined guy? Do you get up every day and 'go to work'?" "Well, yeah. I try to get up every day."
Dick Cavett and Jimi Hendrix

Stop doing stuff all the time, and watch what happens.
Ron Hogan

Winter

GETTING READY FOR THE JOURNEY

You have to leave the city of your comfort and go into the wilderness of your intuition. You can't get there by bus, only by hard work and risk and by not quite knowing what you're doing. What you'll discover will be wonderful. What you'll discover will be yourself.
Alan Alda

INVITING SOLITUDE

In 'Journal of a Solitude', the writer May Sarton describes her quietly determined spiritual and artistic journey. She focuses on the times when she is all alone in her house, in an attempt to get at her 'real' life.

If we are serious about being artists, or about being true to ourselves, I believe that it is essential to spend time alone. Only by spending time alone can we get closer to our own 'real' lives, our own 'real' selves. The world is so noisy – crowded with people's opinions, requests, and demands, the television, the radio, the babble of work, the internet, email, the phone... How can we begin to know who we really are if we don't give ourselves a chance to think without all those other voices ringing in our ears?

But being alone is easier said than done. First there are the practicalities – how do we fit in twenty minutes of sitting quietly when there are three children to look after, and the gas bill needs paying, and the garden is choking up with weeds? How do we explain to our partner that we need to go and do nothing before we ask them about their day?

The second difficulty is that being alone can be an uncomfortable business. The first few minutes of a cup of tea in the garden can be blissful, but then I start to feel guilty about the washing up waiting for me inside. The first day of a week's space can feel luxurious, but then I start to feel a little sad, or a little bored, and I'd much rather go out with my friends instead. Being alone can be uncomfortable because it gives us a chance to get in touch with feelings we may have been tucking away to one side. When there's nothing to hide behind and no-one else to focus on, we may not like what we have to say to ourselves.

So why is it worth persevering? What do we get from letting the uncomfortable feelings arise, maybe writing them down, or simply experiencing them and not distracting ourselves? I can't tell you whether it will be worth it – to answer that question you will have to find your own solitude and see what happens. But I can tell you what I've gained from being alone.

I've got to know myself a little better. I've learnt that I'm prone to fill my schedule to the brim, and that this is not helpful. I've learnt that I find it difficult to just 'be', and that 'getting things done' is something I use to avoid certain aspects of myself. I've learnt that sometimes I hugely enjoy doing nothing. I've been better able to reflect on decisions I've needed to make, and I've had new ideas which have led to new writing. Best of all, I've been able to nourish myself – to give myself some peace. To give myself a chance to let go of old thoughts and let the muddy waters settle. To rest. To be.

If you're interested in what you might learn, start by creating a space for solitude today. Decide whether you'd like to set aside a short amount of time each day, or a longer length of time once in a while, or both. Think about what time of the day would suit you best. Where will you go? What will you do – meditate, write a journal or draw in a sketchbook, go on a fun trip to an antiques shop or a motorbike rally, or just sit and let your thoughts run free? How will you stop yourself from filling this time back up again?

Enjoy getting to know yourself.

Week 14

WATCHING COWS NIBBLING THEIR BREAKFAST

This week I attended a workshop on how to be more authentic. The venue was a grand, shabby old house set in delicious rolling hills and fields of fat cows and clumps of shadowy woods. For the first exercise we were asked to walk out into the gardens and be alone for twenty minutes, and to make ourselves ready for something to 'call to us'. We were asked to come back afterwards so we could share our experiences with the group.

I found a quiet spot on a grassy slope with the hills tumbling down into a valley in front of me. I sat and watched the cows nibbling their breakfast, fiddled with a stick, and waited.

Nothing called to me. I thought instead about what I would say to the rest of the group when I got back, and about what they would think of me. None of us knew each other very well. What kind of impression did I want to make? Which Fiona did I want them to see?

That happens with my writing too sometimes. Instead of it being fun, of being somewhere I can play with words and see what emerges, it becomes 'who do I want everyone to think I am?' What a waste.

I called to myself as I sat on my grassy slope. I said to myself (again) – you are enough. It just takes too much energy to think about which Fiona you want people to see, and you're not fooling anyone anyway. Get on with watching the cows and enjoy it!

Things you might be curious about

Do you ever think so hard about how you'll be 'seen' that you forget to enjoy what you're doing? When does this happen? Who does it happen with? What are you feeling right now?

Suggestions for this week

This week notice when you're making an effort to please someone, or to manipulate the image someone gets of you. Say to yourself 'I am enough' and do it your way instead. See what happens.

We forfeit three-fourths of ourselves in order to be like other people.
Arthur Schopenhauer

Dare to be yourself.
Andre Gide

Week 15

FEELING LOST AND BEING OK WITH FEELING LOST

Over the past few weeks I've taken some time away from my writing. I've made an effort to not fill my diary straight back up again, as I usually would, and so I've had some long expanses of unallocated time. Lucky me, you might say. And yes – lucky me – I am grateful to have the opportunity to do less for a while.

But. But. It certainly hasn't been fun. The longer I spent moodling and pottering and reading the odd page of something or other, the more lost I felt. A little bit of sadness, the odd hint of frustration, but mostly lost-ness.

I'm not sure yet exactly what I'm starting to get in touch with, but I can be sure that it's an authentic part of me. I can be sure that a 'lost me' is more 'me' than a 'busy-all-the-time-and-not-lost me'. That's the important thing for now.

Things you might be curious about

What is it like for you to spend time alone or 'doing less'? What do you think might happen if you gave yourself more free time?

Suggestions for this week

Look in your diary for any opportunities to spend more unstructured time. This time might already be in your diary – you might be checking your emails on your train journey to work, when you could stare out of the window instead. Make a note of any thoughts or feelings that arise, especially if you don't like them!

And this is the simple truth – that to live is to feel oneself lost. He who accepts it has already begun to find himself, to be on firm ground. Instinctively, as do the shipwrecked, he will look around for something to which to cling, and that tragic, ruthless glance, absolutely sincere, because it is a question of his salvation, will cause him to bring order into the chaos of his life. These are the only genuine ideas; the ideas of the shipwrecked. All the rest is rhetoric, posturing, farce.
Søren Kierkegaard

We know little, but that we must trust in what is difficult is a certainty that will never abandon us; it is good to be solitary, for solitude is difficult; that something is difficult must be one more reason for us to do it.
Rainer Maria Rilke

Week 16

TELEVISION AND THE STICKY STUFF

This week I've been on a week-long poetry holiday. We stayed in the playwright John Osborne's house, set in 30 acres of green hills and woods in Shropshire. We were fifteen people who'd never met each other before, and who all thought of ourselves as writers.

There was no TV. Instead we walked down to the lake, read, talked, wrote, picked raspberries, cooked, and sat and looked out over the valley. In one way it was utterly relaxing and rejuvenating – I could feel the peace of the place sinking into my bones. And yet in another way it was utterly exhausting.

We were either alone with our own thoughts, or in a group of 'new' people, wondering what they thought of us, how good a writer they thought we were, how clever a critic. If a fellow writer began to annoy me with their arrogance or a tendency to leave half-empty mugs around the kitchen, there wasn't anywhere to escape to. I was stuck with myself.

I realised how much of an anaesthetic TV can be – how we can use it to give ourselves a break from the hard work of being in a room by ourselves, or with other people. We all use something to escape the uncomfortable, sticky stuff – alcohol, work, exercise, books, partners. What would life be like if we stripped ourselves bare?

Things you might be curious about

How do you protect yourself from the hard work of 'being with other people'? What do you need to restore your balance when it gets difficult – time alone? Time with a hobby? Or do you use 'being with other people' to protect you from the hard work of being alone instead?

Suggestions for this week

Carry a notebook around with you for a few days. When you notice yourself feeling uncomfortable in any way (sad, annoyed, confused, lonely etc.) notice what you do next – turn on the TV, eat a doughnut, call a friend, pick up a book. For the rest of the week, see what happens when you feel sad and you don't turn on the TV or eat a doughnut.

Solitude is the furnace of transformation.
Henri Nouwen

The value of solitude – one of its values – is, of course, that there is nothing to cushion against attacks from within, just as there is nothing to help balance at times of particular stress or depression...
May Sarton

Week 17
EVERYONE IS TALENTED, ORIGINAL AND HAS SOMETHING IMPORTANT TO SAY

When I first read 'If You Want To Write' by Brenda Ueland, it kept making me grin. I re-read it for the third time last week, and devoured it again as if it was a juicy Braeburn apple, smacking my lips every few pages at particularly delicious sentences.

Ueland is especially concerned with making her readers feel good about themselves. She believes that everybody is talented, original and has something important to say. All we need to do is to "break through the shell of easy glibness to what is true and alive underneath". It helps if we surround ourselves with friends and teachers who love us and want to hear more from us. It also helps to avoid "the usual small niggling, fussy-mussy criticism, which thinks it can improve people by telling them where they are wrong, and results only in putting them in strait-jackets of hesitancy and self-consciousness, and weazening all vision and bravery". (She hates critics with a passion!)

This advice applies to people who want to write well, but also to people who want to live well. Here's to cracking open our shells and exposing our brilliant centres!

Things you might be curious about

Do you believe you are talented, original, and have something important to say? If not, what's holding you back from acknowledging this?

Suggestions for this week

Write 'I am talented, original and have something important to say' in your diary or stick it on your fridge. Whenever you read it, note the thoughts and feelings that come up. Do you feel afraid? Inadequate? Disbelieving? Spend a little time with these feelings and try to make friends with them.

There is a vitality, a life force, an energy, a quickening, that is translated through you into action, and because there is only one of you in all time, this expression is unique. And if you block it, it will never exist through any other medium and will be lost.
Martha Graham

Since you are like no other being ever created since the beginning of time, you are incomparable.
Brenda Ueland

FEAR AND TREMBLING

"A further sign of health is that we don't become undone by fear and trembling, but we take it as a message that it's time to stop struggling and look directly at what's threatening us." Pema Chodron

What do we do with fear and trembling? What Pema Chodron is suggesting is that we do the very opposite of what we would usually do. We look it in the eyes. We stand up and walk towards it. We begin a conversation with it and listen to what it has to say.

We might have a fear of being called stupid. We might run away by spending our lives accumulating knowledge, or or by surrounding ourselves with people we believe are less intelligent than we are. We might ignore it by having a little blank when someone tells us they think we've done something wrong. This sidestepping takes a huge amount of energy, like when we're lying on the sofa and we stretch out and stretch out to reach our mug on the table when really we could just sit up to get it. If we are able to face up to our fear, not only will we save all this energy, but we will also learn something important about ourselves. What is it about being stupid that feels so awful?

This concept applies to all kinds of other emotions or thoughts that we'd rather run a mile from. If we feel ashamed about what we said last night, we should walk right up to that shame and examine it. What does it really feel like – hot? Anxious? Is there a hint of anger mixed in? Why might you have made that cutting comment last night – where are you hurting? What do you need?

Our culture doesn't encourage us to approach our fear. It gives us all kinds of toys to help us avoid ourselves – workaholism, drugs, TV, consumerism, an obsession with image. It prefers to give people antidepressants rather than trying to find out why they are sad. It finds displays of emotion worrying, offering a hanky and saying 'there there', rather than 'tell me how it really feels'. And when I say 'our culture', I mean 'you', and I mean 'me'. We are all desperate for things to be predictable, safe and easy. We don't like to see each other's chaos, because it reminds us of our own. And we'd rather that stayed exactly where it was – safely out of sight – thank you very much.

We may feel that if we get closer to our fear and trembling, we won't get out again in one piece. The feelings may crash over us like a tsunami, sweeping us off solid ground and leaving us all at sea. This probably isn't a valid fear, but it might be. It's no good me saying to you 'you'll be fine, just do it'. The difficulty is that we don't know whether it's valid or not until we approach the feelings ourselves.

If you wonder about being overwhelmed, you might want to approach your fear and trembling very carefully, one small step at a time. If you think you might cry forever once you start, give yourself five minutes the first time and then stop. Go to a therapist and build up a relationship that feels safe enough to get you where you need to go. Practise meditation or relaxation exercises to help you out when things get too much. One small step at a time. If you persevere, slowly and surely, then you will find it much easier to live with yourself.

The still lake without ripples is an image of our minds at ease, so full of unlimited friendliness for all the junk at the bottom of the lake that we don't feel the need to churn up the waters just to avoid looking at what's there.
Pema Chodron

Here's to you finding your own still lake.

Week 18

MAKING FRIENDS WITH WHITE CAT, BUT NOT WANTING HIM TO COME INSIDE THE HOUSE

For a year or so a white cat has been hanging around our garden. He's a real bruiser – his face is covered in scars, he walks with a swagger and he hisses a mostly toothless 'hsssssss' if you get within three yards of him.

A few months ago he fought badly with our cat Fatty. He slashed Fatty's neck – there was a pool of blood on the kitchen floor in the morning. White Cat looks completely uninterested if you shout at him to get out of the garden – we had to buy a water pistol as a last resort.

In recent weeks White Cat has started to look old and thin. We slowly realised that he was a stray. I started feeling affection for the old boy. One day I took out cat biscuits and he wolfed them down. Now he's started hanging around our back door with a wistful look in his eyes and making our cats scared to go out. One day he got inside the house and sprayed everywhere.

I sit outside and talk to him a quiet voice. I taste the feeling of caring-for-him and not-wanting-to-let-him-in-the-house.

Things you might be curious about

Look away from the news/the-world-out-there for a second. What is going on in your back yard right now that is difficult? What might happen if you sat with it for a while and tried to make friends with it?

Suggestions for this week

When people talk to you this week about a personal problem they're having, don't try and come up with any solutions. Instead, try and find out what is so difficult for them. If they've been unhappy at work for a while, rather than talking about job adverts ask them why it feels so difficult to leave. Ask questions and listen. Encourage them to stay with their difficulty. Alternatively, have the same conversation with yourself about one of your own problems.

The truth of the thing is not the think of it but the feel of it.
Stanley Kubrick

Fear is a question: What are you afraid of, and why? Just as the seed of health is in illness, because illness contains information, your fears are a treasure house of self-knowledge if you explore them.
Marilyn Ferguson

Week 19
THE MIRROR OF SOMEONE ELSE

A few weeks ago our neighbours were playing their music very loud late at night. I started to worry about my partner getting angry with them – maybe he'd go round and shout at them, or be in a bad mood all evening.

I've noticed this happens quite a lot – something will happen and I'll worry about him or someone else getting annoyed or bored. I started to wonder if there was something else going on as well.

How did I feel when my neighbours played their music loud? Actually, now I come to think of it, I felt a little bit annoyed as well. And what are the implications of me getting a bit annoyed? I HATE being annoyed with people – it means I have to face up to confrontation or sit with feeling angry, yuk.

And so came the horrible realisation – whenever I worry about someone else being annoyed (or bored, or not liking someone etc.) it's because I'm annoyed or bored or don't like someone. How annoying!

Now whenever I have these thoughts about someone else I ask myself (sometimes with my teeth clenched) what is it I'm not 'owning' here? What am I seeing about myself in the mirror of someone else?

Things you might be curious about

Who really annoys you? What are they telling you about yourself? You'll know you're there when you get to the 'ouch'!

Suggestions for this week

Choose one trait that often annoys you in other people – for example arrogance, or neediness. Carry a little notebook around with you for the week, and jot down every time you notice yourself exhibiting this trait. At the end of the week, read over what you've written down. If you didn't spot yourself being arrogant or needy very often, then you need to look harder! How do you feel about yourself when you re-read your notes? How could you start to make friends with the arrogant or needy parts of yourself?

Everyone you meet is your mirror.
Ken Keyes Jr.

I can't help detesting my relations. I suppose it comes from the fact that none of us can stand other people having the same faults as ourselves.
Oscar Wilde

Week 20
AHA!

I've recently started monthly 'creativity meetings' with my friend Esther so we can support each other's writing. (They also seem to involve nice pub lunches, all in the name of nourishing our muses, of course. I can highly recommend the sticky toffee pudding in the Catherine Wheel in Goring.)

This month I talked about the difficulty I've been having with my current novel. I've been nagged by a constant feeling of frustration that I'm not able to get the first draft down any more quickly, and it's getting in the way of the writing.

As I talked (helped along by questions from my friend) I tuned in to a feeling of 'falling forwards' but never quite landing. I realised with an 'aha!' that a part of my frustration is located in 'wanting to get to the end of the story'. It's a similar feeling to waiting for the first glimpse of the sea on a day out, or to the end of an anecdote you're telling a friend, but on a much bigger scale.

At the end of our meeting the frustrated feeling was still there. But I was also much clearer about where this feeling came from, and what it was about. As a result I felt differently about the feeling. That is already making it easier to enjoy the journey, rather than constantly craning my neck to try and see a sparkling blue strip on the horizon.

Things you might be curious about

Is there a feeling/thought you've been feeling/thinking for a long time that's difficult to live with? Could you find out more about this feeling/thought? How?

Suggestions for this week

Choose a confusing thought or feeling you'd like to get closer to. Ask a friend to listen to you talk about this thought/feeling for twenty minutes – asking you questions or clarifying what you're saying but not giving you any advice. Alternatively write in your journal for twenty minutes on this subject. What came up?

Inside yourself or outside, you never have to change what you see, only the way you see it.
Thaddeus Golas

Perplexity is the beginning of knowledge.
Kahlil Gibran

Week 21
OUR SCREWED-UP BITS

I worked for some time as both a coach and a therapist. Both involve 1:1 work with people who are 'stuck' with something, with the hopeful intention of moving things forwards in some way, but the relationships are set up very differently.

In therapy the boundaries are very solid, with regular weekly face to face sessions that start and finish on time, and little or no sharing of my own experience. The coaching relationship is much more like the relationship you'd have with a colleague at work – I shared my own experiences much more freely, the sessions were often less frequent and over the phone, and I could meet up with coaching clients socially without compromising the work.

For a long time I thought that the coaching work was 'lighter' – we didn't go so deep, and I wasn't holding the same kind of responsibility that I had for my therapy clients. I was, however, battling with a sense of unease about my coaching practice, and for a couple of years I tried to work out what my problem was.

It was a long time before I realised that as a coach, I was presenting myself as someone who could 'fix things', rather than as someone who was willing to be alongside someone as they struggled with their own difficulties. This hooked into a part of me that was prone to taking on inappropriate responsibility (a screwed-up bit!). The coaching work was actually 'tiring me out' much more than the therapy work.

The difficulty is in working out which of our 'screwed-up bits' can be exploited in a way that's good for us, and those that get us 'hooked in' to something that's not good for us, whether in our career, our relationships or our habits. Complicated stuff and a vague gut feeling might be the best information you get to start with. If it's important, the feeling won't go away until you've worked it out.

Things you might be curious about

What screwed-up bits are you aware of in yourself? (Obsessive tidiness, needing to be helpful, a hatred of arrogance etc.) When do these get 'hooked into' in your career/relationships at the moment? Does this 'hooking in' feel helpful (working as a PA and exploiting your 'tidiness') or unhelpful (working for charity and wearing yourself out with your 'needing to be helpful')? What changes would make things easier on you?

Suggestions for this week

Pay attention to any vague uncomfortable gut feelings you get this week. Give them a little more space to speak up – write them down, talk about them, or just listen more closely.

To every disadvantage there is a corresponding advantage.
W. Clement Stone

There's a period of life when we swallow a knowledge of ourselves and it becomes either good or sour inside.
Pearl Bailey

SEARCHING FOR MEANING

I'm prone to ending up in the kitchen at dinner parties. I don't enjoy being in large groups, and it's helpful to fill up other people's glasses and put olives into little bowls while I get my bearings. It gives me a purpose, and I feel useful.

Life is a huge dinner party that goes on and on, and none of us really know why we've been invited. Does the host think we'll get on well with Bob now we're divorced? Do they enjoy our jokes? Are we just there to make the numbers up? Even when we do know what's expected (by our parents, our culture, our government...) do we agree?

Viktor Frankl, who survived the concentration camps to become a great philosopher and psychotherapist, thought that "those who have a 'why' to live, can bear with almost any 'how.'" He suggests that we are always free to find our own meaning, no matter how restrictive our circumstances are. We can do this through being creative, taking pleasure from nature, working out what we enjoy giving, learning about ourselves and others, and a myriad of other activities that don't depend on our environment.

If we can find meaning in our lives, then we have a golden thread to return to when the ride gets bumpy. Any large project is more manageable when we have an idea of where we're heading. If we're saving money for a trip to Iceland, not going out for a meal feels like a step towards the icebergs rather than simply being denied a good lasagne.

Different people will approach meaning in completely different ways – one may be motivated to study to be a doctor to help sick people, and the other may want a good wage so they can enjoy fine wines and a cottage in the country. Both reasons are good reasons, but we need to make sure we're finding our own purpose and not someone else's. So where do we begin to search for our own meaning?

It may be useful to look back at our lives so far, and to think about when we were particularly satisfied with events or relationships. If you list these events you may start to find a common thread – you were able to encourage someone else to achieve something wonderful, or you got pleasure from other people's responses to your work. Finding meaning isn't always about helping other people directly – it may be the satisfaction you get from solving a maths problem, or the pleasure of learning about yourself in relationships.

It might also be useful to think about who you admire. Is it your old teacher for her academic sharpness? A colleague for his determination to learn from all the misfortune that came his way? What is it about these people's lives that have meaning? How could you harness the same principles in your own life?

The expectations of the people around us and of society often get in the way of our search. Our parents might disapprove of our desire to become a taxidermist, and society might not sanction our desire to quit our prestigious job to live on less money and spend more time with our family instead. The influences of others can be subtle yet powerful, and may lead to a great deal of conflict between wanting to live your life in a meaningful way, and wanting to be approved of.

Searching for our purpose is a lifelong task, and it is likely to change along the way as we learn about ourselves and the world. But even when we have a vague idea of what we're here to do, everything else in our lives will begin to fall into context. Does this situation help you with your quest, or distract from it? What about this relationship? A search for meaning can help us to live lives that fit us like a glove.

Week 22
THE DIFFERENCE BETWEEN GUT AND OUGHT

Before I started writing my third novel I had all kinds of fancy ideas about what it ought to be about. I was interested in the complex dynamics between men and women, the politics of the female body, the cultural context of the 1960s.

I've almost finished my first draft, and the book seems to be about none of these things. My main character, Violet, has told her own story instead. She's said the things that she wanted to say. She's been allowed to say these things because I've trusted that my unconscious knows better than the 'ought' part of me that decided on my clever-clogs themes.

I sometimes see my unconscious as a huge compost heap, with me chucking in the raw materials (experiences, books, conversations) and it doing all the hard work. It composts away out of sight – making sense, processing, breaking down and building up. It prods me in the right direction by giving me a feeling in my gut. When I start writing I might think I want to grow a rose, but it always knows better and grows raspberries instead, or a spiky thistle.

Things you might be curious about

Do you know the difference between your gut and your ought? In which situations have you been able to give your gut a say? How did this work out for you? How could you give your gut a little more space (except for loosening your belt)?

Suggestions for this week

Practise listening to your gut by: writing down your dreams, asking yourself 'what would it be like if I wanted/believed the opposite?', listening to the feelings in the pit of your stomach, asking yourself questions (out loud or writing them down), turning your head quickly and catching sight of your reflection in other people.

As soon as you trust yourself, you will know how to live.
Johann Wolfgang von Goethe

Our life is composed greatly from dreams, from the unconscious, and they must be brought into connection with action. They must be woven together.
Anais Nin

Week 23
THE SECRET OF LIFE

I caught a bit of 'City Slickers' this week, a film about business men reconnecting with their purpose on a cattle-driving holiday. At one point 'city slicker' Mitch Robins (Billy Crystal) and tough-old-cowboy trail boss Curly (Jack Palance) do some bonding out on the range. Curly shares his philosophy with Mitch, commenting that city slickers spend fifty weeks of the year 'getting knots in their rope' and think that two weeks of playing cowboy will untie them. Their conversation went something like this:

Curly: Do you know what the secret to life is?

Mitch: No, what?

Curly: This. (holds up one finger)

Mitch: Your finger?

Curly: One thing, just one thing. You stick to that and everything else don't mean noth'n'.

Mitch: That's great, but what's the one thing?

Curly: That's what you got to figure out.

An unlikely place to find a philosophy for life, but it stayed with me as I wondered what my 'one thing' was. What do I need to do or become or make or find that has incredible meaning to me?

The closest I can get to my 'one thing' so far is 'to help the truth be heard'. At the moment this is my thing as a writer and therapist and also personally. There are other important themes in my life, but for me this is the golden thread that runs through everything. While I am engaged in this process, everything else slots into place.

Things you might be curious about

What is your one thing? Are you already engaged with it? If you don't have a clue, what would help you get closer to discovering it? If you are already engaged with it, how could you increase your commitment to it?

Suggestions for this week

Try and get closer to your one thing by: asking three friends what they think your one thing might be, remembering the dreams you had as a child, listing all the things in your life that you get the most satisfaction from, imagining your ideal job, thinking about how you'd like to be remembered by family, friends and colleagues.

Blessed is he who has found his work; let him ask no other blessedness.
Thomas Carlyle

Nothing contributes so much to tranquilizing the mind as a steady purpose – a point on which the soul may fix its intellectual eye.
Mary Wollstonecraft Shelley

Week 24

WANTING TO DO IT ISN'T ENOUGH

I've just seen an interview with Charles Dance, a British actor. He's directing his first film, and his interviewer was asking him whether or not he was going to return to acting.

He said he was looking forward to acting again, and spoke about what acting meant to him. He said that it was something he needed. He said that if you wanted to be an actor, it wasn't enough to want it – you had to need it. He said that without it he felt incomplete.

I feel that way about my writing. At the moment other priorities in my life are keeping me away from any proper writing, and I feel the same tug that Charles Dance is speaking about. The process of writing isn't always comfortable, and I often wonder where I'm going with it. But there's never a question of whether or not I should carry on. The question instead is how do I ensure the long-term survival of my space for writing? What should I be doing right now to feed my muse? It's never a question of whether I should be a writer, but of how.

Things you might be curious about

Is there a need in you for anything? If you don't have needs, how can you nourish your curiosities and your wants and see what they grow into? If you do need something (caring for children, making beautiful things, learning physics, creating gardens) how do you currently honour this need?

Suggestions for this week

How could you honour your needs in a small way today and every day this week?

What makes the engine go? Desire, desire, desire.
Stanley Kunitz

Often people attempt to live their lives backwards; they try to have more things, or more money, in order to do more of what they want, so they will be happier. The way it actually works is the reverse. You must first be who you really are, then do what you need to do, in order to have what you want.
Margaret Young

Week 25

THIS ONE'S FOR YOU, JOHN

On October 24th, 2004, the radio DJ John Peel died of a heart attack at the age of 65 whilst on a working holiday with his wife in Peru.

I've been quoting John as my all-time-hero since I was 13, when I used to listen to his deep, bumbling, comforting voice on headphones in bed late at night.

John Peel played exactly the kind of music he wanted to play, from plinkerty plunkerty country and western to screaming thrash metal to pumping drum and bass to bubblegum Japanese pop to... you get the idea. He was well-known for making mistakes on air and regularly played music at the wrong speed or mislaid the next record. He often spoke with great love of 'The Pig', his affectionate nickname for his wife Sheila, and of his four children.

I loved John Peel because he was an ordinary man who achieved the extraordinary, simply by doing what he loved to do. He just kept on quietly searching for new music that electrified him, and shared it with us in the hope that we might be electrified as well.

Here's to you, John. Rest not in peace but in the glorious noise of all that life-giving music.

Things you might be curious about

What will people remember you for when you die? What would you like them to remember about you?

Suggestions for this week

Make a small commitment to doing more of what you love doing: book a regular slot in your diary, look at volunteering, start planning a career change, open a savings account, buy a new notebook and start recording your ideas for poems.

A lot of people say – "You've been kind of instrumental in the career of..." They always mention Led Zeppelin for some reason, but I don't think of it in those terms. I don't do what I do either to win praise or fame for myself, but because I like doing it. And if other people like the music that I like, then that's even better.
John Peel

Bugger... wrong speed.
John Peel

Moodling

Week 26
FEEDING YOUR CREATIVITY

An engineer emailed me a few weeks ago and said that being creative worked as a boost for him in his job. Being able to play around with concepts and see things in a new way complements his more analytical, meticulous and rigorous way of working.

He also noticed he tends to 'run out' of this creative juice and asked for some suggestions to keep the creative spring welling. Good question!

I can only speak from my own experience of feeding my creativity. I've learnt some things as I've gone along, and I'm still learning. I need blank space every so often – ten minutes in the garden with a cup of tea every day, and the odd blank day. I need to be able to follow my nose when I get curious about things – I've just started learning Russian, and have been reading a pile of books about gardening. I need to spend time with other creative people. I need train journeys. I need to write in my journal every morning. I need to have some fun every so often; get my toes muddy in the garden or try on posh hats. And I need to be kind to the creative side of me – reassuring it when it gets rejected and reminding it of its successes.

That's what my muse asks for, but yours might like something else entirely, like train-spotting or growing marigolds. When it's next hungry, see what you can tempt it with.

Things you might be curious about

How do you know when you're feeling less creative? How does this affect your work/your personal life?

Suggestions for this week

Make a list of twenty things you suspect may feed your creativity, e.g. starting a scrapbook, collecting egg cups, going swimming, walking your dog, listening to a new radio station, making your own wrapping paper, reading autobiographies of creative people, singing in a choir. Commit to doing three of these things this week.

Creativity means to push open the heavy, groaning doorway to life. This is not an easy struggle. Indeed, it may be the most difficult task in the world, for opening the door to your own life is, in the end, more difficult than opening the doors to the mysteries of the universe.
Daisaku Ikeda

Nature and its colorful glory or cities and the nitty-gritty – freeways or even empty parking lots – all are waiting to inspire the muse.
Randall Sexton

Spring

CHANGING DIRECTION

And the day came when the risk to remain tight in a bud was more painful than the risk it took to blossom.
Anais Nin

REDIRECTING ENERGY

If we've cleared a space, approached our fear and trembling and moved closer to an idea of what's important to us, then what next? Unless you're already spending your life in exactly the way you want to be spending it, then it may be time to redirect some of your energy. When I say energy I mean all kinds of different energy, including physical and mental energy, time, money, possessions and relationships.

Energy is our main currency. It gets us up from the sofa when there's a trashy afternoon film on, and stops us from staying under the duvet all day. Everything we do in life requires a dollop of it. A friend is only a friend because we've already invested energy into the relationship. We'll use physical energy to write them a letter and post it, emotional energy to let them know how happy we were to see them last week, and financial energy to buy the stationery and the stamp. We may have an expectation of getting some energy back (a letter in return) or we may get some energy from the writing itself (a good feeling from the knowledge of how happy our friend will be to receive it).

It's important to pay attention to where our energy ends up, because it's a limited resource. Doing the right things with our energy may make it go further, like squeezing the last squidge of toothpaste from the tube. But although most of us could climb an average-sized mountain or swim a reasonably small channel if we put enough energy into the training, it's unlikely that we'd be able to do both in the same afternoon.

It can be useful to look at our relationship with the limited energy we have available to us. We can make a note of what activities or people drain us like bloodsuckers, and notice when we feel full of zing. We can become aware of when we feel dissatisfied about 'wasting our energy', and be curious about why we keep going back to waste some more. We can draw a little pie-chart to work out whether we're putting the right proportions of energy into the most important areas of our lives.

We can also find out a lot about our relationship with energy by looking at how we deal with money, which some people see as 'solidified energy'. We swap our time, mental and physical energy for money, so what do we do with it when we get it? Do we hoard it all away and find it difficult to enjoy it? Do we spend large amounts of it on impulse or use it to try and cheer ourselves up or bolster our self-esteem? Do we have energy leaks because we're always late doing our tax return or because we buy too many bespoke suits and never wear them?

Once we're clear about where our energy is going, it may be useful to reflect on why we're using energy in this way. How did our family relate to money, or to energy? What might we be avoiding? How do we feel about scarcity? How do we feel about abundance? What problems do we think we'll be solving if only we had more money/time/physical energy?

When we understand where and why our energy is getting wasted the leak may fix itself, but it might also need some work from us. It might require us to make changes to our routine, our relationships, or our job. We might need to spend time with some difficult feelings. If it's an old and rusted-up issue, we might need to get in an expert.

Our energy is all we have, and is far too precious to waste. Get out your spanners and inspect your plumbing!

Week 27
A PUNNET OF CHERRIES

Money. Where to begin? I could easily write a musing about money once a week for the next year and still have more to say.

I've just come back from a spare hour walking around some clothes shops. I'm on a budget at the moment, and I only have a certain amount of money to spend each week.

As I tried on various clothes, I made an internal decision – 'I'll allow myself an extra £20 this week because I'm working hard', and then 'I can use next month's spare money today' and by the end of my bargaining I'd allowed myself £50 to spend on whatever I wanted.

Luckily I came to my senses before I actually got to the check-out, by remembering that I'd enjoy spending it more when I actually had it to spend. I also realised that I was in a state of mind where the spent money would be 'gulped' money, like when you eat something so quickly you don't really taste it.

I've been eating my £2 punnet of cherries since I got back. That's about 10p per sweet, tart, juicy fruit. And they're good for me. And they're a gorgeous shiny deep red. I was in a rich man's world all along!

Things you might be curious about

How much pleasure do you get per pound/dollar? Where do you 'gulp' your money and forget to taste it properly? How aligned is your spending with your long-term goals and/or the things you get meaning from?

Suggestions for this week

Spend a week writing down where you spend your money on non-essentials and noticing how much you appreciate these 'treats'. Did everything you buy feel 'worth it'? If not, how could you avoid spending this empty money again?

To fulfill a dream, to be allowed to sweat over lonely labor, to be given the chance to create, is the meat and potatoes of life. The money is the gravy. As everyone else, I love to dunk my crust in it. But alone, it is not a diet designed to keep body and soul together.
Bette Davis

He who distinguishes the true savour of his food can never be a glutton; he who does not cannot be otherwise.
Henry David Thoreau

Week 28
SPENDING YOUR ENERGY WISELY

Earlier in my career I worked as a coach, and for a few years I spent a great deal of energy on marketing my services. At the time I thought it was a sound investment, but I gradually started to feel like I was chucking my energy into an abyss. Not only was I getting fewer clients than I'd expected, but something else didn't feel right. I wasn't getting any 'feeling-good-about-what-I'm-doing' energy back as I went along.

It encouraged me to revisit my reasons for wanting to be a coach, and my rationale for focussing on the coaching business as a way to earn my living. I realised that I was using the coaching to protect myself from failing at what really mattered – my writing, and my work as a therapist.

Once I was clear about this misdirected energy, I was able to harvest whole bucketfuls of energy to send to the things closer to my heart. My therapy practice blossomed, there was plenty of space for my writing, and with a little creativity I was able to earn as much money as I needed without spending any time as a coach. Phew.

Things you might be curious about

Where does your energy come from? How could you get more? What in your life deserves more energy than it's currently getting? Are there any energy leaks?

Suggestions for this week

Make a commitment to pull some of your energy back this week, by saying no to something, or by approaching a task with a different attitude. Notice the energy you release as a result and direct it towards something that you're passionate about.

I merely took the energy it takes to pout and wrote some blues.
Duke Ellington

Time is the coin of your life. It is the only coin you have, and only you can determine how it will be spent. Be careful lest you let other people spend it for you.
Carl Sandburg

Week 29
HOVERING IN DAYTIME TV LAND

Today I found it impossible to get down to any work. I aimlessly browsed the web for a couple of hours, checking my email every three minutes to see if any new ones had come in. Eventually I turned off the computer and watched daytime TV. You know the sort of thing – how to redecorate your bedroom for 25p, and interviews with ex-soap stars currently doing panto at Skegness.

Hovering in daytime-TV-land is worse than not working. It's not relaxing either.

Eventually I summoned up the energy to switch off the TV and sat in silence for five minutes with nothing to anesthetize me. I asked myself what I needed, and what I wanted to do next.

I might have decided to take an hour or an afternoon off, and properly enjoy it. I actually decided that I wanted to write this musing, and then go out to the bank. So here I am.

Things you might be curious about

Do you ever hover in daytime-TV-land, which is neither working/being productive nor relaxing/playing? When are you especially prone to this? How could you shift this time into either proper work or proper relaxation?

Suggestions for this week

Try and catch yourself slipping into this mode and stop to ask yourself what you really want to do. If your choices are limited, be creative. If you're stuck at work, could you face some routine filing? Could you make coffee for your team? Give yourself permission to do it.

A good rest is half the work.
Yugoslav Proverb

Work is not always required. There is such a thing as sacred idleness.
George MacDonald

Week 30
ON BEING SPOILT

I'm still living on a budget. What seems to work best for me is putting a certain amount of cash into my wallet every week. I spend this on meals out, earrings, fudge and other inessential items. If I want anything bigger then I put money aside until I've got enough.

I cheated this week. I was on Amazon buying a present for a friend, and I just happened to see a book I wanted. 'Click' – it was mine. If I spent another £10 I'd get free delivery, so 'click' there's another, but oh I'm still £2 away from free delivery... 'click'!

The world we live in makes it easy for us to cheat. We can get three years' interest free credit on sofas, bigger mortgages than we can really afford... every other day a letter drops onto our doormat offering us money – yes, you'll have to pay it back at inflated rates, but you can have it now!

Having a certain amount of money in my wallet each week works for me because it forces me to make a choice about what I most want or need. It reminds me in a small everyday way that all of our resources are limited, and that I'm lucky to have what I have. We all make choices every day about where we spend our money, our energy. We all want to buy into the myth that we can have whatever we want, and more. But there's something strangely satisfying in being clear about what I have and saying no to myself. If I 'pay myself back' for those books over the next few weeks, I'll treasure each poem in them all the more. I'll savour every word.

Things you might be curious about

What is your relationship with 'limited resources' like? Do you want to believe that you can have whatever you want? How does it feel when you acknowledge your limits?

Suggestions for this week

Decide on a budget for yourself this week – using money or something else that is valuable to you. Notice what it's like when you can't have something that you want, or you're forced to make a choice. If you don't stick to your budget, try again next week, and keep noticing how it feels.

Seek not, my soul, the life of the immortals; but enjoy to the full the resources that are within thy reach.
George Pindar

If you know how to spend less than you get, you have the philosopher's stone.
Benjamin Franklin

TAKING RISKS

The whole point of risk is that it might involve us coming to harm or losing something valuable. Sometimes the danger is mostly imagined or out of proportion – we may feel terrified about getting into a car for the first time after we've been in a crash. But the tricky thing about risks is that there always is a real chance that something will go wrong.

We live our lives with 'low level risks' constantly in the background. We can't get out of bed in the mornings without risking falling over the cat. We're in danger of a tin of paint falling on us when we walk underneath a ladder. Every road is a potential hazard. Most of us are willing to accept these risks and get on with our day-to-day living, becoming fleetingly aware of them from time to time (maybe when our friend falls over his cat). Life is risky enough already. So why make things worse for yourself and try something new on purpose?

Taking risks is a way of expanding our options. If we take a risk successfully (i.e. nothing goes horribly wrong) then choices that were previously 'out of bounds' become a possibility. Taking risks that might seem minor to other people can make a big difference to our lives. If we're brave enough to say 'no' to a friend who wants us to look after their scary dog, we have the option to say no again – to looking after the scary dog, or to going to see Jon Bon Jovi with them. Risks are usually most scary the first time, and when we say no and our friend doesn't slap us and the world doesn't end, we'll feel more comfortable about making our needs known again.

If the worst usually doesn't happen, then what stops us from taking risks left, right and centre? Unless you're the type who spends their weekends abseiling or hiking through the wilds of Peru, we are mostly creatures of habit. On the whole, we like predictable outcomes – we like to know where we are and what we're doing. Even hikers in Peru like to have their lucky pair of pants with them, or know that their husbands are waiting for them at home. None of us like to be taken by surprise, or to be dropped into unfamiliar situations. We might get hurt, embarrassed, tricked, afraid, shouted at, or savaged by flesh-eating Peruvian beetles.

Our scariest risks will vary depending on what our 'worst thing' is. For some of us being rejected is the ultimate danger, and we will tie ourselves up in knots to make sure that we're always agreeable, and avoid conflict like the bubonic plague. For other people, being tied down might be the worst thing, and we might get palpitations at the thought of getting a mortgage or going on a fourth date.

We'll usually have very good (if out of date) emotional reasons for our fears. When we were small we might have picked up that our mother was unpredictable, and spent the rest of our childhood looking for something reliable to hold on to. If we experienced violence in the home, we may spend the rest of our lives smoothing out arguments between other people, desperate not to be in that powerless place of being a child in a war zone again. Children don't have the choices adults do – to say 'stop it' or to just walk out, and so difficult situations really can feel like 'life or death'.

It can be useful to know about our own worst things. We're more likely to understand why we go pale when we think of taking our driving test – failing always was ridiculed in our family. And if we understand, we're more likely to be compassionate with ourselves, and to give ourselves a break.

This is one of the ways we can support ourselves to take risks. We can also make sure we have cheer-leading friends and family around us, take risks one small baby step at a time, choose our timing, and remember why we're taking the risk in the first place. Then we can squeeze our eyes shut tight as we step off the edge...

Week 31

WHY I SHOULD HAVE TAKEN A GRAPE

I'd prefer train journeys if everyone else in my carriage kept their mouths closed. No over-excited children, no slightly sloshed football fans, no friends gossiping about who snogged who last night. Nice and quiet so I can read my book or gaze out of the window without having my attention snagged by someone else.

I was settling down to a journey to London this week when a girl in her early twenties sat down next to me with her mobile. She spoke into it loudly, saying something rude about the people in the seats behind us that I'm sure they heard. Half-way through the journey, when I was lost in labyrinths of thought, she nudged me gently on the arm. 'Do you want one?'

She held a bunch of grapes out towards me. I did want a grape. I was thirsty, and they looked plump with juice. But before I had a chance to think about it I was shaking my head, smiling, saying no. The bit of me that is afraid that people will talk too much, the bit of me that hasn't the energy to summon a fake smile and fake interest, shut the possibility down.

I might have taken a grape and gone back to my dreaming. I might have started a conversation with this girl and discovered that we both loved Raymond Carver, or walking in the mud without any socks and shoes.

Things you might be curious about

When do you turn down opportunities before you've even given yourself a chance to consider them? What are you protecting yourself from? How could you start to risk yourself, just a little bit, in that area?

Suggestions for this week

When you say 'no' this week, become aware of the things you might be protecting yourself from. These might include: change, being out of your depth, being seen by someone else as failing, seeing yourself as failing, anger (yours or someone else's), sadness (ditto), being rejected, getting close to someone, losing security, going mad, falling over etc.

Listen, are you breathing just a little, and calling it a life?
Mary Oliver

I want to stay as close to the edge as I can without going over. Out on the edge you see all kinds of things you can't see from the center.
Kurt Vonnegut

Week 32

HOW TO FOOL YOURSELF INTO DOING SOMETHING SCARY

I'd written poetry for many years before I started to think about writing my first novel.

My poems contain 15 or 100 words each, so I started by asking an editor friend how many words there were in an average novel. She said about 80,000.

80,000! And then there was the plot, creating believable characters, finding the time to write, handling dialogue... how does anyone ever write a novel?!

I wondered how I could get around these huge fears and write it anyway. And so I decided that I would write a novel as an experiment. I wasn't going to create a masterpiece, or find a £100k publishing deal, but I would put 80,000 words down, one after the other, and see what I ended up with. At the very worst I'd gain the experience of writing a novel, and learn a bit about writing along the way.

It worked, and 80,000 words and a few revisions later an agent was interested enough to want to see it again after a re-draft. Once again terror descended on me – I was writing for someone... what if they didn't like the changes I made? Who did I think I was? But in order to get the work done I had to put those thoughts aside, and pretend that I was a novelist.

I'm now working on my third novel, and it's still scary – but I'm still tricking myself and the work is getting done.

Things you might be curious about

What are you putting off because it feels insurmountable? What if you did it anyway and 'failed'? How can you remove some of the pressure?

Suggestions for this week

Choose a small difficult task, or a small chunk of a large task, and play around with it in your head until it becomes more manageable. Get it done.

The question should be, is it worth trying to do, not can it be done.
Allard Lowenstein

Hope begins in the dark, the stubborn hope that if you just show up and try to do the right thing, the dawn will come. You wait and watch and work: You don't give up.
Anne Lamott

Week 33
SQUASHING HOPE

I've just sent off my poetry manuscript to a publisher I'd love to be published by. I've been aware of a rising hope in me, like a child who can't wait for their birthday/trip to the beach/new Teenage Mutant Ninja Turtle toy.

Is it helpful for me to give this hope some space inside me, or should I squash it and be more 'realistic' instead?

I spoke to a friend about this and he asked me if I had a choice. Wasn't the hope already in me? Wasn't I asking myself whether or not I should pretend it wasn't there? We also spoke about the risk inherent in hope – the risk that your dreams will be dashed, that you'll feel the full force of disappointment like a shove in the chest, ouch.

I'm still pondering, but so far I'm acknowledging that the hope is already there, and enjoying it if I can, without going off on frequent hour-long fantasies about life as a famous poet. Disappointment will come, and that's part of the deal. I'll do my grieving if and when I need to. I'm trying to abandon myself to the highs and the lows, and to suck the marrow from every single minute.

Things you might be curious about

What are you holding back from experiencing? What is it that's stopping you from engaging with this experience more fully? What would it be like to enter into it a little further?

Suggestions for this week

Are you pretending not to feel something this week? Disappointment at the way a friend has let you down, fear about a job interview, pleasure that a hated colleague is in trouble? Open yourself up to hearing more about these feelings. See what happens when you get acquainted.

The advantage of the emotions is that they lead us astray.
Oscar Wilde

Accept everything about yourself – I mean everything. You are you and that is the beginning and the end – no apologies, no regrets.
Henry Kissinger

Week 34
DIVING INTO THE BLUE

Something I tend to do is to consider the person I'm with (are they hungry? are they looking sad? did I just annoy them?) before I consider myself.

This makes it difficult for me to work out how I'm feeling when I'm with someone else. I take my eyes off myself and look over every few seconds to check whether they're bored yet or whether they want to say something.

Recently I managed to feel a feeling and just keep going, like diving down into the blue. I managed to hold my breath (by not checking the person who was listening to me) for a couple of minutes.

I could hold my breath for this long because this person has listened to me, consistently and reliably, for years. I was able to trust their ability to look after themselves, and their desire to see where I might go with my feeling, even if it got dark and murky and there were spiky fish with googly eyes.

Maybe I'm beginning to learn that I can breathe underwater after all.

Things you might be curious about

Which relationships in your life help you to take risks? What stops you from asking these people for help? When these people give you opportunities to take a risk, do you take them?

Suggestions for this week

Identify an area in your life where you've been afraid of taking a risk. Think about the people around you. Who might be able to support you in taking this risk, either practically, physically, emotionally or financially? Make a list and ask three people for their help this week.

There is no such thing as a 'self-made' man. We are made up of thousands of others.
George Matthew Adams

We do not believe in ourselves until someone reveals that deep inside us something is valuable, worth listening to, worthy of our trust, sacred to our touch. Once we believe in ourselves we can risk curiosity, wonder, spontaneous delight or any experience that reveals the human spirit.
e.e. cummings

COMMITMENT AND RESILIENCE

If we become clear about how we construct our meaning and what we really want from life, does achieving our goals become effortless? Well – not really. That's not been my experience, anyway. Knowing what we want is only the beginning of the journey, like seeing a photo of lemon trees in Sicily and deciding to grow your own. You still need to sell your house, buy some lemon seeds, learn Italian, break the news to your mother-in-law and get pet passports for your five Chihuahuas. It isn't likely that all of these tasks will be a piece of cake, lemon or otherwise.

If you want to get things done, one of the qualities you'll need to nurture in yourself is an ability to keep on plodding forwards, no matter what gets thrown at you. Lemon trees are more expensive than you thought? You'll do extra shifts at work for the next year. Your partner isn't keen? You'll make sumptuous lemon cheesecakes and drop hints about siestas and fine Sicilian wines. But how do we develop resilience? What makes one person able to scale Mount Everest, and the next nervous about facing the bathroom scales?

Our capacity to stick with something will partly depend on our past experiences of commitment. Were we encouraged to struggle on when we first tried to tie our shoe-laces, or did mum take over too soon? How did our parents deal with their own set-backs? Were we rewarded for trying and trying again, or punished for not getting it right first time?

It's never too late to improve our resilience. We can encourage ourselves by acknowledging the times we've persisted, whether or not we were successful. You might have asked your boss for a rise, and been assertive during the conversation about why you feel you deserved it. You might have managed to complete a course on cake decorating, despite feeling like you'd never learn to control your icing bag or master the arts of marzipan. You might have fixed the leak in your manifold. These are all examples of times when you didn't take the easy option and go and watch TV instead, and should help you to see yourself as someone who is capable of persevering.

It might help to collect stories of people who have succeeded against all the odds. Who do you admire in your personal life or in the world of sport or art? Talk to them or read interviews and biographies about them – how do they keep going when things get difficult? What do they say to themselves when they're told 'no' for the six hundredth time?

You can also improve your resilience by getting in touch with what you're afraid of. What might happen if you did keep trying and still didn't make it? What would the worst case scenario be? If you're afraid of failure, why does it matter so much? If you're afraid of what other people might think, what kind of feelings does this bring up in you? What do they taste like? What do they remind you of? Getting to know these feelings will help you lessen the risks of persevering.

How do we know when we should quit? This is a difficult question, because sometimes even when everyone (including us) thinks it's time to give up, the solution may be just around the corner. On the other hand, we don't want to dedicate our entire lives to becoming an opera singer if our voice boxes aren't designed to hit the high notes. Maybe all we can do is gather feedback from people we respect and trust, and examine the situation as objectively as we can. How much is it costing us to keep trying? How long has it taken other people to become successful in the same field? How important is it for us to succeed? The most useful information may be a vague feeling in our gut that we want to give it one more year, or that we need to look again at our goals and maybe try an orange orchard instead.

Successful people will lecture you about the importance of determination until the cows come home. Rather than beating yourself around the head, develop a curiosity in your capacity to keep going. What helps you? What hinders you? Acknowledge your strengths and weaknesses, speak to yourself encouragingly and make the most of what you've got.

Week 35

EVERYTHING IS ALREADY PERFECT

My friend Patrick subscribes to the theory that everything is already perfect.

He doesn't mean that life isn't full of supermarkets that run out of your favourite yoghurt, or partners that don't change the toilet roll, or any of the more difficult, spiky, horrible things that strike us all without any warning.

He means instead that all of these things can be viewed as an opportunity to learn valuable lessons about ourselves. They can strengthen the bits of us that need strengthening, and endow us with compassion, gratitude or patience. They can also point us towards something that needs our attention, like a sprained ankle telling us we need to slow down a little.

My book was rejected by five publishers last month. It's been a painful process – I felt each criticism like a stab to the heart, I began to doubt the validity of what I'd written, my creativity dried up and I couldn't get on with my writing.

After a while I returned to the creativity books I've always found helpful. I gained some distance and thought about how I felt and why. I've come out the other side with a much healthier view of 'what people say' about what I've created, and more confidence in my work. Most importantly, I've started writing again. I wouldn't have strengthened this part of me if it hadn't been for the rejections, and I'm glad I have. If I'm going to carry on writing then you can be sure I'll need it again.

Things you might be curious about

How do you respond to the suggestion that everything is already perfect? What might happen if you opened your mind to your experiences a little further?

Suggestions for this week

Choose a recent situation that you have felt is unpleasant or unfair (choose something small before you work your way up). If you looked at it and believed it to be 'already perfect', what benefits might there be to you? What parts of it did/do you especially struggle with? What does that tell you about yourself?

Life has no other discipline to impose, if we would but realize it, than to accept life unquestioningly. Everything we shut our eyes to, everything we run away from, everything we deny, denigrate, or despise, serves to defeat us in the end. What seems nasty, painful, evil, can become a source of beauty, joy, and strength, if faced with an open mind. Every moment is a golden one for him who has the vision to recognize it as such.
Henry Miller

When you realize how perfect everything is you will tilt your head back and laugh at the sky.
Buddha

Week 36

AM I REPEATING MYSELF?

Sometimes when I write these musings I feel as if I'm saying the same things over and over again. Simplify your life. Concentrate on the details. Make friends with your feelings. Create space. On and on and on like a broken record.

I realise that it's because these are the things I most need to hear myself – the things that are the biggest challenge to me. I learn these lessons over and over because, for whatever reason, they're difficult lessons for me to learn.

Maybe the realisation that we're repeating ourselves can help draw attention to the fact that we need to listen to ourselves more carefully.

Maybe the realisation that we're repeating ourselves can help draw attention to the fact that we need to listen to ourselves more carefully.

Things you might be curious about

When people come to you for advice what do you suggest they do? Can you notice any themes in what you say? Do you need to tell yourself these same things? How could you listen more carefully to yourself?

Suggestions for this week

Write yourself a list of the lessons you need to remind yourself of again and again and stick it inside your diary or above your desk. Read it daily and reflect on how you did yesterday. Remember to be compassionate with yourself. These lessons might include: be kind to yourself, don't jump to conclusions about other people, don't eat too much chocolate when you're feeling sad, listen to your body and rest when you're tired, don't offer to help automatically, be honest with your partner, don't take it personally...

All truly wise thoughts have been thoughts already thousands of times; but to make them truly ours, we must think them over again honestly, till they take root in our personal experience.
Johann Wolfgang von Goethe

Any ideas, plan, or purpose may be placed in the mind through repetition of thought.
Napoleon Hill

Week 37

STRENGTHENING THE THREAD

When you're hanging on by a thread, identify that thread and do all you can to strengthen it. Gardening is my thread, consistently providing therapy through years of ups and downs. If this blink in time seems a bit crazier, well, perhaps it is. Gardening serves as a gentle reminder that the wheel turns and seasons come and go, each filled with its own impossibly tender beauty. So maybe it's time to go outside and look for tulip noses poking through the damp earth and reaching into the winter mist.
Sally Basile

It takes a certain amount of oomph (grit, guts, spunk, zest, what wonderful words!) to keep these threads going. I know that writing is one of my threads. A couple of weeks ago I stopped my usual writing-first-thing routine. I thought I'd have less resistance to writing now I'm on the second draft of the novel. I thought I could easily do an hour in the afternoons or before lunch.

I thought wrong. Starting on Monday I'm returning to my hour-first-thing routine. It takes effort to get it done, but I can measure the payback in truckloads. It holds me together. It reminds me who I am. And it brings me as much joy as Sally's glorious tulips.

Things you might be curious about
What are your threads? How do you honour and strengthen them?

Suggestions for this week
Set some regular time/energy/money aside to invest in your threads, starting from this week. Examples are: ten minutes of reading poetry every morning, booking two trips a year to an important building, writing daily emails to a friend, creating a new space for your model aeroplanes, starting a course on plastering, buying a new sketchbook, finding a second hand bike.

The habit of love cuts through confusion and stumbles or contrives its way out of difficulty, it remembers the way even when it forgets, for a dumfounded moment, its reason for being. The path is the thing that matters.
Eudora Welty

Keep busy with survival. Imitate the trees. Learn to lose in order to recover, and remember nothing stays the same for long, not even pain. Sit it out. Let it all pass. Let it go.
May Sarton

Week 38

ON A LACK OF BLAZING MOMENTS OF BRILLIANCE

I write 'morning pages', an artist's tool recommended by Julia Cameron and Roselle Angwin which asks you to write three pages of whatever comes off the top of your head first thing in the morning every morning. Over the past few months I've become more and more frustrated with myself.

I fill page after page with petty worries about lack of money and lack of time and the eczema on my hands and lack of money and lack of time and…

Where are the slices of pure brilliance? When will I dazzle myself with a description of the flame-bellied robin I saw in a January tree? When will I imagine stories about magic stags and enigmatic princesses in deep green forests? When will I turn the sound of the rain into a poem?

Instead I obsess about the state of my hands, how much time and money I've got, time, hands, money… there's no space for anything else.

A few times I've caught myself being boring and have tried to force something more interesting out, but the writing has always been stilted, inauthentic. The truth is that first thing in the morning I am full of these everyday worries at the moment. In the past few weeks I've settled down into feeling more OK about what I write. Yes – I still annoy myself. Maybe if I stay with my feelings for long enough, green shoots will start growing out of the worried landscape. Or maybe they won't. At least it's my landscape.

Things you might be curious about

Which parts of yourself are you less comfortable with? Which parts do you long to change? Could you experiment with acknowledging these parts of yourself rather than fighting against them? Could you find a space for them to just 'be'?

Suggestions for this week

When you feel frustrated, bored, annoyed, disappointed or disapproving about yourself this week, stop and notice what you're feeling. Write down everything you feel, e.g. 'I'm pathetic, I shouldn't be so weak, I remind myself of my uncle' etc. When you've written down everything you can think of, put this piece of paper aside and revisit what originally caused you to feel bored, annoyed etc. Can you relate to this part of yourself with any more compassion?

The courage to be is the courage to accept oneself, in spite of being unacceptable.
Paul Tillich

One must also accept that one has 'uncreative' moments. The more honestly one can accept that, the quicker these moments will pass.
Etty Hillesum

Moodling

Week 39
WAITING FOR THE URGE

I have always hated doing domestic chores around the house, especially hoovering. I put things off until they absolutely have to be done. I resent these tasks because I'm usually far too busy doing 'more important things', or trying to snatch some time to relax.

Recently I've had much more free time at the weekends. Gradually I started to feel bored during the afternoons, and eventually I woke up one morning thinking 'I could clear out that corner today'. The urge to clean arose naturally, from the middle of plenty of blank space.

There are some jobs we'll never have the luxury of 'waiting for the urge' for – filling in passport application forms, brushing our teeth, taking out the rubbish. But if it can wait, give yourself lots of space and you never know... the urge might come!

Things you might be curious about

Do you ever give yourself enough time to get bored and then feel the growing urge to get something done?

Suggestions for this week

Give yourself as much blank space as you can this week. Don't put any pressure on yourself to do anything unnecessary. See what happens.

There are pauses amidst study, and even pauses of seeming idleness, in which a process goes on which may be likened to the digestion of food. In those seasons of repose, the powers are gathering their strength for new efforts; as land which lies fallow recovers itself for tillage.
J. W. Alexander

Sometimes the most urgent and vital thing you can do is take a complete rest.
Anon

Summer

ENJOYING THE RIDE

I cannot believe that the inscrutable universe turns on an axis of suffering; surely the strange beauty of the world must somewhere rest on pure joy!
Louise Bogan

ENGAGING WITH LIFE

When I say engaging with life, I mean getting up so close to it that you can feel the tiny hairs on its cheeks and smell its slightly garlicky breath. I mean living without anything between us and the world – taking off our layers of clothing one by one and standing naked and doing a little dance, even if we can't dance for toffee.

I won't need to give you much encouragement to engage with the lovely things in life. Take deep gulps of freshly-baked-bread-smell, concentrate on the silky smoothness of the skin in front of your partner's ear, notice the feeling of satisfaction when you've finished five loads of washing – aaaah. We're still mostly pretty rubbish at it, but more of that later. Why would we want to engage with the yucky stuff? Why would we want to pay more attention to the black mould behind the sink or to the sinking feeling in our stomach when we look at our bank statement?

In my experience, if we don't engage with the yucky stuff then it tracks us down anyway, like a slightly incompetent private detective. Not only that, but it takes up bucket-loads of our energy into the bargain. It uses up energy as we turn our heads on crowded trains to see if it's sitting behind us, and as we drive the long way home in the hope of shaking it off. If you're trying to avoid something unpleasant, you might get caught with your pants down and you might not, but there's certain to be a cost to you either way.

Engaging with the yucky stuff will help us to live with ourselves and with other people. If we are able to be honest with ourselves about our little penchant for cheating, we might be able to smile wryly at ourselves when we get caught for not buying a parking ticket, rather than getting furious at the parking attendant and avoiding that area of town from that day forth. We might also feel a little more compassionate towards our friend when we find out the present they 'bought us' was actually an old Christmas present from Grandma Doris.

It might also help us to work out what we need. If we swallow down our loneliness and keep it in the pit of our stomach, we won't understand why we cry at a children's programme about a lonely penguin, and we'll spend our energy unconsciously changing the subject every time loneliness comes up in conversation. If we're able to open ourselves up to our loneliness, we won't just start feeling our own sweet sadness. We'll also be able to start working out why we don't already have more friends.

So what is it that gets between us and life? How are we keeping ourselves protected? We devise all kinds of clever unconscious tricks to protect ourselves from the yucky stuff – choosing a certain kind of friend who won't ruffle our feathers, saying no to invitations that might take us closer to the darkness. All we can do is be curious about ourselves – why did I get so angry when he said I was clever? Why did I have an overwhelming urge to eat ice-cream after listening to that song? Detached curiosity will help us start peeling back the layers and exposing some of our more vulnerable bits to the fresh air.

How can we move in closer to the good stuff? One way is to move in closer to the yucky stuff. A head full of worrying about our current performance as a project manager is sure to get in the way of us feeling the cool sand between our toes. Another way is to learn how to share our good stuff with other people, and to find ways of accepting what they want to give us. Finally, we can try and remember that life doesn't go on forever, and stop drifting off. As Natalie Goldberg says, "The sad thing is that the knowledge of impermanence is often not enough for human beings. We have to hit ourselves over the head."

We need to keep hitting ourselves over the head if we want to suck the marrow out of life. We need to remind ourselves that this particular sunset is unique, and that we might only have another 1,537 left to see. We need to keep death close if we really want to throw our arms around life.

Week 40

THE BRAIN IS A WONDERFUL ORGAN

As the poet Robert Frost said, "The brain is a wonderful organ. It starts working the moment you get up in the morning and does not stop until you get into the office."

My worst days are just like that – I start the day with the end already in mind, as if the hours in between are just something to get through. It's not really living, it's 'waiting for the work-day to be over'. What a waste.

What helps is to remind myself to enjoy the day 'as I go along'. I might make time to read something nourishing at lunchtime, or go and chat with a colleague I haven't seen for weeks. I might simply notice the clear winter light streaming in through the windows.

It also helps to take more of myself to my work. I might not be looking forward to that dry seminar, but at least I can speak up with some questions of my own. If I've got to deal with that difficult colleague, at least I can try and really listen to what they're saying. When I take myself along, passing the time becomes less like wading through mud and more like feeling it squidging between my bare toes.

Things you might be curious about

When do you have a tendency to leave your brain behind? What might you be missing out on? What helps you to reconnect with what you're doing?

Suggestions for this week

Choose an appointment or a commitment that you're not looking forward to this week. How could you take your brain along? Ideas are: sit down beforehand and write a list of things you might learn, say something you're slightly nervous about saying, be curious about what you're thinking and feeling, take a friend along, listen really carefully to other people, be playful, notice your surroundings, take a risk.

The best way out is always through.
Robert Frost

Some rainy winter Sundays when there's a little boredom, you should always carry a gun. Not to shoot yourself, but to know exactly that you're always making a choice.
Lina Wertmuller

Week 41
POTATOES AU GRATIN... MMM

Last week I mentioned to my partner that my friend Heather was coming over and I didn't know what I was going to cook. When I arrived home with her he'd made us the most delicious dish of potatoes in cream, garlic and blue cheese that I've ever tasted. And my friend brought me a bunch of irises with sunny yellow streaks on velvety dark purple petals.

For me these are the kind of 'ordinary favours' that Sharon Salzburg is talking about in her quote below. I didn't ask for the potatoes or the flowers. My partner and my friend didn't have any expectations of what I'd give them in return. They just wanted to make me happy.

I'm conscious of how rarely I 'compassionately reach out' to people in my everyday life. A lot of different things get in the way. I don't have much time or energy or money, and fear that there might not be enough to go around. I'm preoccupied with myself for some reason or other. I'm worried about how my gift might be received. I forget.

Then I remember how easy it is to reach out. How little it costs to smile at a mother pushing her baby down the street, to slip a little note into our partner's wallet to tell them how much we care, or to give an old book to a friend who might appreciate it. All we need is a thimble-full of the desire to make somebody happy.

Things you might be curious about

What gets in the way of you giving to other people? What could you do to start removing these barriers? What might happen if you shared a little more?

Suggestions for this week

Do three 'ordinary favours' this week – choose three different people and choose three different gifts. Don't expect anything back, except the delicious knowledge that you're planting those seeds.

Any ordinary favour we do for someone or any compassionate reaching out may seem to be going nowhere at first, but may be planting a seed we can't see right now. Sometimes we need to just do the best we can and then trust in an unfolding we can't design or ordain.
Sharon Salzberg

He who obtains has little. He who scatters has much.
Lao-Tzu

Week 42
WARM LAPS AND TICKLED EARS

I work in a lovely Victorian building, with comfy sofas and high ceilings and a huge blowsy garden. This week I was sitting downstairs and chatting with a colleague when a black and white cat appeared at the doorway.

He came straight over and with minimal encouragement jumped onto my lap and got stuck into the serious business of getting his ears tickled. You could hear his purring from across the room. He had the right attitude – wander into open doors, seek out warm laps, and jump right up.

Things you might be curious about

What or where are your warm laps? How does your attitude help/hinder you in your quest to get your ears tickled?

Suggestions for this week

Ask three people for something you want. See what happens.

Mama exhorted her children at every opportunity to 'jump at de sun.' We might not land on the sun, but at least we would get off the ground.
Zora Neale Hurston

Don't ask yourself what the world needs; ask yourself what makes you come alive. And then go and do that. Because what the world needs is people who have come alive.
Harold Whitman

Week 43

DAVE AFTER 63 YEARS IN THE SAME JOB

This week I was lucky enough to meet Dave, who has been gardening for 63 years. He first went out with a spade as an enterprising twelve-year-old, and dug his neighbour's gardens for a few coins, or for a cup of tea and a sandwich. He made enough money to pay for a trip to cinema, and a bonus bag of chips if he'd had a good week.

Ten years past retirement age and he's still working seven hours a day. He's been looking after the same private gardens for twenty years now – when he started they were just a bare patch of earth. He took me to see them and they were stunning – acres of glossy shrubs and bright flowers and smooth lawns and elegant trees, all planted with an eye for colour, size, texture and overall perspective.

Dave has never earned very much from his work. He's never been 'promoted' and he's never had a company car. His employees rarely appreciate all the different jobs that are necessary to keep their gardens looking wonderful – as he said, they'd only notice if he stopped doing them for a few months.

He works because he loves to. Because he's still learning. Because he has high standards and takes pride in seeing the results. Because a robin has recently taken to perching on his wheelbarrow and getting a free ride. Because he loves to stand at the top of the gardens at first light and look out over them and drink in their beauty.

Things you might be curious about
Do you feel the same way as Dave does about your own work? Why not?

Suggestions for this week
Think about the work you're currently doing (this doesn't have to be paid work – include anything you do that gives your life meaning, including raising children or making art). If you don't already feel like Dave, what can you do this week to help you to love your work? What can you do this week to start your journey towards the work you'd love to do?

A man doesn't learn to understand anything unless he loves it.
Johann Wolfgang von Goethe

Derive happiness in oneself from a good day's work, from illuminating the fog that surrounds us.
Henri Matisse

SLOWING DOWN

Stand in a doorway on a busy pavement in a city at rush hour. What do you see? I see a stream of people moving along the street like a thousand-legged, thousand-headed insect, their eyes fixed straight ahead, their little legs taking them along as quickly as they can. Where are they hurrying to? Why are their faces so blank? Why do they look so annoyed when an old lady steps out in front of them and bends down to talk to her beagle? Now look at your own life. Are there any similarities? Maybe you like living your life in the fast lane. Why would you want to slow down anyway?

The pleasures of slowing down are all in the details. Look up – what beautiful pale stone carvings above that shop full of washing machines. That woman's hair is the colour of chestnuts, and just as glossy. There's a ladybird, climbing up the wall of the bus shelter. And the freesias get a chance to release their scent when you linger in front of the florists.

Slow food tastes better. You'll eat less of it if you're really concentrating, and it doesn't give you indigestion either. Slow conversations, peppered with comfortable silences, take us to depths that hundred-miles-an-hour-chatter never can. Even slow washing up allows us to watch dollops of bubbles break free and float in the air, and to savour the satisfaction of dripping, squeaky-clean plates. And I don't have to spell anything out when it comes to slow kisses.

The pleasures of slow are also in allowing calm to seep into you, like pale blue ink onto a sheet of blotting paper. Slowing down allows a little space inside you, so you can ponder in a more relaxed way about a difficult customer at work, and realise that your colleague will know what to do. Slowing down will allow that idea about starting a new business, which has been stuck under a pile of worries about your day job, to rise up into your consciousness like a sunny bright yellow helium balloon.

A little more space and sharper details are also the downside of slow. If you walk a little more slowly, you might see that homeless person sitting in a doorway and catch his eye for a few seconds. You might remember that you are unhappy in your relationship, and that you vowed to yourself you'd leave by the end of last month. You might really notice the pain in your lower back. Yes – back to the yucky stuff again.

Slowing down allows us the space to feel the things we need to be feeling, and so if you cancel half your appointments and start to feel sad rather than wonderful, then that's a good thing too. Your sadness might have waited a long time to surface, and it might have a bit of catching up to do. Whatever you're feeling right now is a good thing to be feeling, whether it's pleasant or not.

So how can we practise the art of slowing down? Being engaged in something slow can help, and gardening is the perfect example. We can't persuade a tomato into ripening if there isn't enough sun, and if the mice eat all our sweet-pea seedlings we can't try again until next year. Attending to the rhythms of nature can remind us to wait, to be patient, to accept a slower pace. We can schedule in 'time to be slow' – ten minutes in the morning when we're not allowed to rush about, or a week in a country cottage with not much to do. We can learn to catch ourselves when we're getting tangled up, and take three deep breaths or go outside and look at the sky for thirty seconds. We can surround ourselves with slow-motion people. We can go through our schedules with pruning shears and ruthlessly cut out anything that doesn't earn its keep.

Life easily sweeps us up into busyness, like stepping out onto a crowded pavement. We might think that if we decide to slow down to a stroll, people will bump into us and give us dirty looks. Some probably will, and they'll have their own reasons for walking as fast as they can, looking straight ahead. But some might slow down with us. They might even stop and sit with us at a pavement café, for some lazy conversation, hot chocolate, and a croissant with blackcurrant jam.

Week 44

A POCKETFUL OF SEEDS

Last week the afternoon light on the trees was the colour of honey. I heard a man talk on the radio about the old 'scientific' experiments to give dogs electrical shocks until they became helpless. I noticed that the plants in the office looked so plasticky that they only accentuated the dry air, characterless furniture and fluorescent lights. I read a gut-wrenching poem by a poet I didn't know, Marie Howe, and wanted to read more.

I often 'catch' details like this that have the promise of making it into my writing, or being something I could learn from. I see them as seeds – unformed ideas that have the potential to grow into something bigger if they're watered and given time.

I try to save these seeds now – by writing them down in my diary, or by filing them away in an index card box I've covered in tiny silver stars. I also try to put time aside to have a look at them and see if any need germinating. Most of them go mouldy in time and get thrown away. But occasionally one grows into a whole orchard of apple trees.

Things you might be curious about

Do you notice seeds when they arrive? What do you do with them? Do you give them a chance to germinate and grow?

Suggestions for this week

Collect five seeds this week (anything that interests you – a book review, a sketch of a rabbit, a snippet of an overheard conversation about soap, an idea for redecorating your bedroom). At the end of the week, put aside time to have a look at them, and put one of them into a pot with some compost.

It is like the seed put in the soil – the more one sows, the greater the harvest.
Orison Swett Marden

To live is so startling it leaves little time for anything else.
Emily Dickinson

Week 45

THE IMAGINATION WORKS SLOWLY AND QUIETLY

Brenda Ueland told us that "The imagination works slowly and quietly". I love this phrase. When I read it right now, what is it telling me?

It is telling me to say no to that new project I've been involved with. It is saying I need to turn my computer off at the weekend. It's whispering into my ear that what I'd really love to do is to cancel my plans and sit in a café with my notebook all afternoon instead.

Things you might be curious about

How much space do you give your imagination? What gets in the way of your ability to think creatively?

Suggestions for this week

Make a date to go and lie down under a tree, sit on a park bench, drive through the countryside, take a seat in a café or run on the beach this week. Let your imagination off its leash.

I am enough of an artist to draw freely upon my imagination. Imagination is more important than knowledge. Knowledge is limited. Imagination encircles the world.
Albert Einstein

The sea does not reward those who are too anxious, too greedy, or too impatient. One should lie empty, open, choiceless as a beach – waiting for a gift from the sea.
Anne Morrow Lindbergh

Week 46
DARKNESS AND LIGHT

The main character of the novel I'm working on at the moment is a 62-year-old gardener called Leonard. In preparation of bringing him to life I've been meeting with gardeners and this week I met Steve, head gardener at Calke Abbey in Derbyshire.

Themes emerged in our conversation, and I recognised them from talking with other people working on the land. There was a sense of being closer to the earth – the weather, the animals and birds, the needs of growing things. There was also a sense of slowness – a feeling of being grounded. And everything was brought to life by a sense of being tuned in to the constantly changing seasons. Daffodils wouldn't be so bouncingly spring-like without pared-down winter, and when the visitors start arriving at the beginning of a new season it's all the sweeter for the gardens having been closed and quiet.

I'm looking forward to the colder weather coming – I'll be getting out my woolly hat and gloves again, and waiting for the white sparkle of frost and puffs of cotton-wool breath. I'm looking forward to cocooning myself with chestnuts and afternoon films in a warm house. Half of the pleasure is in knowing that the cold will pass.

Things you might be curious about

How aware are you of the passing of time in your own life? When are you more likely to forget and think instead that you've got all the time in the world?

Suggestions for this week

When you're engaged in your favourite things this week (eating a ripe earthy mango, having a conversation with your three-year-old nephew, driving at 70 miles an hour with your window down) remind yourself that your experience is transitory. Watch your favourite things get even more delicious.

At Christmas I no more desire a rose
Than wish a snow in May's new-fangled mirth;
But like of each thing that in season grows.
William Shakespeare

All things are only transitory.
Johann Wolfgang von Goethe

Week 47

I AM WRITING, I AM WRITING, I AM WRITING

When I had a proper day job it used to take me twenty minutes to walk to the office from my house. Some days I'd leave the building at the end of a long day feeling like I couldn't bear to wait twenty minutes to get home (with a little stamping of my foot).

Over time, I learnt to play a little trick on myself whenever this feeling arose. I'd somehow manage to forget that I was impatient to be home, and just carry on walking. Before I knew it I would be turning the corner into my road.

This week I've been practicing slowing down and paying attention. I've been holding 'I am walking' in my mind (like a pebble in my palm) when I'm walking, or 'I am washing up' when I've been washing up.

This morning I was driving. I brought my attention back from thinking about my tax return and was suddenly aware of my body speeding along over bumps and round corners at 50 miles an hour, inches from the ground. Wheeee!

Things you might be curious about

When are you prone to waste your time by living for the future or through the past? How could you remind yourself to slow down and engage in the present moment again?

Suggestions for this week

Practise saying 'I am driving' to yourself when you drive this week, or 'I am eating', or 'I am listening to my partner'. See what happens.

That we find a crystal or a poppy beautiful means that we are less alone, that we are more deeply inserted into existence than the course of a single life would lead us to believe.
John Berger

By taking one thing at a time, and being mindful of our state of mind, we can simplify the business of life.
Norman Fischer

BEING HERE

Being here sound easy. Aren't we all already here? Where else are we? Where are you right now? You might be paying attention to these words with all your concentration, or you might be thinking instead of what you'll have for dinner later. You might be replaying an argument you had with your partner last night, and trying to work out how you were right. You might be imagining bumping into that sexy filmstar in the local supermarket and them asking you back to their place for a glass of wine.

We spend most of our time not quite in sync with what's happening right now, like a wrist watch with a mind of its own. What is happening right now will often trigger off thoughts and feelings about relationships, events and ideas from the past. These thoughts and feelings then get all tangled up with the present, like when our partner gives us some useful feedback and we suddenly see our critical father and shout 'you can't stop telling me what to do!' We also like to take refuge in fantasies about our future, especially when we'd rather not face the realities of what's happening right now. Why make the effort of going to auditions when we're going to be spotted on the street by a top model agency any day now?

Our minds also have the tendency to get caught up in what we'd like to be seeing, rather than what's actually there. Life is a slippery beast, and we like to hang onto firm structures and beliefs about how things work so we don't slide off the back of it altogether. We like to know that we have firm ground under our feet – that we love raspberry cheesecake, for example, or that our friend Bob is always reliable.

We'd rather the ground was firm even if we don't particularly like the beliefs we have. We'd rather hold onto the knowledge that we're 'stupid' despite frequent evidence to the contrary, because having to adjust our view of ourselves is pretty scary stuff. If we don't even know whether we're clever or stupid, then what does that mean about everything else we thought we knew? Do we have to start getting to know ourselves again from the very beginning? Not knowing 'who we are' is terrifying, because without 'who we are' we don't even exist.

Although we'd rather not admit it, the ground is always moving. Our friend Bob said he'd meet us at five and then didn't turn up until six twice last week, even if we did tell him it was probably our fault. And we didn't enjoy that cheesecake much last week, or that slice the month before, even if we did blame it on a dodgy recipe at the time. The alternative is not knowing who Bob is, or not knowing how we can give ourselves what we want to eat.

The advantage of being able to let go of these certainties is that we'll be more able to see things as they really are. Letting go of our old beliefs will help us to welcome a truer sort of truth. We can see Bob as a normal human being with all the usual human frailties, and ask him why he was late, and he can confide in us that he's having problems at home. We can realise that cheesecake is too rich for us these days, and that we actually prefer a nice raspberry sorbet. As Pema Chodron said, "the truth you believe and cling to makes you unavailable to hear anything new.".

Letting go of imaginary solid ground helps us to be here. So does engaging with life and slowing down. What else can we do to bring ourselves back to the present? We can set our alarms twice a day, and stop whatever we're doing to pay attention to the here and now. We can be curious about the thoughts that keep pulling us backwards or forwards – ruminating on an old painful relationship, or fantasising about our future as a rock star. We can 'be here' during a single task each day – getting out of bed, or drinking tea.

Being here is about paying attention to each moment as it runs through our fingers. It isn't about catching hold of these moments, or looking away when we'd rather have something different. It's about how things really are right now. Being here now is the only chance at life we have.

Week 48

LOOKING AT THE BUTTERCUPS

A therapist friend of mine was talking today about how few clients she has at the moment. At first she worried about it as she usually did, wondering if she'd be able to pay the bills and when she'd get busier. Then she decided she was going to enjoy the quiet instead – spend more time in the garden, recharge her batteries.

It reminded me of a conversation I had with my agent last week. We were talking about how long it might take to get published, and she urged me to make the most of my pre-publication stage. No book tours to get in the way of the writing, no publisher putting pressure on me, no colly-wobbles about how the book might be received.

A year ago I would have thought 'yes that's all very well, but I want it now!' I would have thought that everything would be solved once I had a book published – all my anxieties about the quality of the work, all my financial worries, all my difficulties balancing writing with the rest of my life. But now I am ready to understand what she's saying.

It's not that I don't want it any more. I'm still channelling plenty of energy in that direction. It's not that it won't be wonderful when it does happen. I just know now that my current set of worries and difficulties will be replaced by another, different set. And as Anne Lammott pointed out, "if you're not enough before the gold medal, you won't be enough with it."

For now I know that I'm walking in the right direction. I know that my first published book is going to be a beautiful landmark – a crumbling castle or a waterfall. I'm not sure how far I've got to go, so for now I'll enjoy looking at the ladybird crawling across that glossy leaf, those bright buttercups sprinkled beside the path.

Things you might be curious about

What are you impatient for? What do you think 'getting there' might solve? What would it be like to shift your focus to enjoying the journey instead?

Suggestions for this week

Choose an event or a situation you've been 'pinning your hopes onto' – buying a new house, finishing (or starting) a relationship, having more money, getting a new job, finding the right pair of shoes for the party. Write a list of the things you imagine it will 'fix'. Now take each item on the list and see how you can start working on each item right now. If you think having a new house will mean you can make new friends, join a club in your local area instead, or be curious about why you don't have more friends already. If you think glam new shoes will make you more popular, then ask all your friends what they like about you instead, or buy a book on improving your self-esteem.

If the path be beautiful, let us not ask where it leads.
Anatole France

Ten thousand flowers in spring, the moon in autumn,
a cool breeze in summer, snow in winter.
If your mind isn't clouded by unnecessary things,
this is the best season of your life.
Wu Men

Week 49
GIRL ON A SPACEHOPPER

My partner is in a field somewhere on a scooter rally this weekend, so I've spent two days immersed in my novel re-write. One of my characters, Ruth, uses photographs as a way of stilling her mind – she chooses one at a time and meditates on them as if she were looking at a candle or a sunset. I wanted to share this one with you – it was taken by Siirka-Liisa Konttinen in Newcastle in 1971. I'm hoping you're all familiar with Spacehoppers? Over to Ruth.

"This evening I looked at a photo called 'Girl on a Spacehopper'. She has her back to us so it's difficult to work out how old she might be – maybe seven or eight? The photographer caught her mid-bounce, suspended above the empty concrete and brick streets.

She's wearing a long sequin-ed dress with a big bow on the back over her pale woollen jumper, and the full skirt has swallowed the Spacehopper whole, you can only see a thin slice of circle poking out beneath it.

Her head has moved too quickly for her hair and it floats around her as if the air were water. Strands of it are clumped together into rat-tails and point in different directions. It could do with a brush, but she doesn't care what she looks like, she doesn't care if a dress-strap has fallen from one of her shoulders. She's bang in the middle of her experience of bouncing. She's jumping for joy."

Things you might be curious about

What types of experiences do you feel bang in the middle of? Something creative? Laughing with friends? Tickling your dog's muzzle? How could you do more of this stuff?

Suggestions for this week

Put some time in your diary this week to do something that will make you jump for joy.

And forget not that the earth delights to feel your bare feet and the winds long to play with your hair.
Kahlil Gibran

When you do things from your soul, you feel a river moving in you, a joy.
Rumi

Week 50
IT HAS TO BE MADE, LIKE BREAD

Love doesn't just sit there, like a stone; it has to be made, like bread, remade all the time, made new.
Ursula K LeGuin

I think you could substitute a few other words for 'love' and this quote would work just as well – happiness, money, success, friendship.

I love what it's saying, and at the same time I resist it a little. Surely the whole point of working towards something is that you get to keep it? Surely once my books are written, I get to look at them stacked up and say 'I'm a successful author'? Surely working hard will give me the money to buy a cottage in the country where I'll live happily ever after?

A part of me already knows that I'll only ever be as successful as my last book, my last review, the laughter or boredom of my last reader. I know that my cottage in the country might have dry rot. I know that I'll have to continue re-inventing myself, feeling vulnerable, taking risks. Maybe the really good stuff comes when our hands are aching from kneading.

Things you might be curious about

How do you feel about the prospect of all that kneading? Where do you get your kneading-energy from? Where could you get more?

Suggestions for this week

Choose one area of your life that's got a little stale – an old friendship, a neglected border in the garden, a passion you've been too busy to indulge. Do a little kneading.

Human beings, by change, renew, rejuvenate ourselves; otherwise we harden.
Johann Wolfgang von Goethe

Peace does not mean an end to tension, the good tensions, or of struggle. It means, I think, less waste. It means being centered.
May Sarton

Week 51

A BLACK CAT AND A POT OF TULIPS

Yesterday I was sitting in the garden and the sun was singing at the top of its voice. I looked over to see that my cat was sitting right next to my small deep blue pot of bright red tulips. It was as if he'd considered the garden as a whole, tried out a few different positions, and settled on the exact spot where the glossy blackness of his coat perfectly balanced out the blue and red splashes.

Unless I'm under-estimating his sense of colour co-ordination, it seems unlikely that he really chose that place to sit just so I could look at how handsome he was. But I wish you could have seen it. And the violent yellow colour of rapeseed against the blue sky as I drive to work. And the cream and terracotta pattern of bricks on the house opposite. And... And...

Things you might be curious about

What can you see (feel/smell/taste/hear) right now that is beautiful?
What can you see (feel/smell/taste/hear) in the next ten minutes?
Go there now!

Suggestions for this week

Soak yourself in beauty this week.

Beauty in things exist in the mind which contemplates them.
David Hume

I thank God for most this amazing day:
for the leaping greenly spirits of trees and a blue true dream of sky;
and for everything which is natural which is infinite which is yes.
e. e. cummings

Moodling

Week 52

THE SEA, THE TEA, THE SPARKLY FLIP-FLOPS

Last weekend my partner and I camped on a field behind my friend's beach-hut for a birthday party on the beach. I've been going back to this place for fifteen years, and spent several blissful summers there as a teenager, bang in the middle of friends and beer and boats and bonfires on the sand.

On the morning after the night before, I struggled out of our hot tent with my notebook. I walked round the hut and onto the cool sand. A friend appeared like magic and brought me hot sweet tea before disappearing. I sat on a chair in the middle of the empty beach, wearing my new blue-and-green sequin-covered flip-flops. The sun was blaring like a radio. The water sparkled in front of me, making a thousand plishing and shushing sounds. And I wrote.

I wrote well. A few new poems were born. I felt like I could have written forever.

Things you might be curious about

How are you different in different environments? Where are the places that help to suck creativity out of you? What do you like to be surrounded by – grass? Buildings? Deer?

Suggestions for this week

Find a new place that inspires you. This might be under a tree in your garden, or it might be an hour's drive away. Claim this place as yours – sit down and do some thinking, or write a letter to someone, or do some sketching. Promise yourself you'll return.

There is no need to go to India or anywhere else to find peace. You will find that deep place of silence right in your room, your garden or even your bathtub.
Elisabeth Kubler-Ross

You must have a room, or a certain hour or so a day, where you don't know what was in the newspapers that morning... a place where you can simply experience and bring forth what you are and what you might be.
Joseph Campbell

THE END OR
THE BEGINNING?

I don't know where I'm going, but I'm on my way.
Carl Sandburg

Unless you've skipped ahead to this bit, you've been on a bit of a ride over the past weeks, months or year. What has it been like for you? Did you manage to ask yourself all the questions? Which bits did you think were irrelevant to you? Were they really?

If anything in this book has made you feel a little bit uncomfortable, then good. A little bit of feeling uncomfortable or anxious or sad or annoyed is a sign that something is shifting. If these were easy questions, then we would have already found all the answers and got on with living a perfect life.

If you haven't felt uncomfortable, then that's fine too. In my experience, words have a tendency to seep into us when we're not looking, and lie underground until we're ready to listen to them. Be curious about what happens over the next few months. Do you keep remembering one of the quotes in this book? Do you start noticing something about yourself that you hadn't noticed before? Keep listening. See what unfolds.

These questions are only intended to be the beginning of something, or more accurately, to put you in touch with something that has already been there for a long time. You'll have heard all these ideas before – as Montaigne said "I have only assembled a bunch of other men's flowers, providing of my own only the string that binds them together". Only you can give them the power to change you.

I hope that you continue the journey, by looking up a book that interests you in the resources section, carrying on with your journal, getting some therapy, starting something creative or just putting five minutes of 'musing time' aside a day.

I hope your curiosity has been piqued.

Thank you for having me, and go well.

Resources section

THE MAGIC OF MORNING PAGES

Morning writing centres me, clears the pond scum off the surface of my mind, plants my feet firmly on the ground and gets me out of my own way.
Eleanor Blair

I've carried out a certain ritual every single morning for the past few years. It takes half an hour, and it brings me clarity, 'aha' moments, relaxation, stability, and helps me to stay in touch with the source of my creativity. It works like magic.

This ritual is Morning Pages. Morning Pages are three pages of flow-of-consciousness writing with my beautiful silver fountain pen, into an A4 spiral notebook, morning after morning. Some mornings they're full of my aches and pains and complaints about having to get out of bed and feed the cats. Other mornings I remember the shocking pink flowers I spotted the day before, or describe the river I swam across in my dream. Whether I'm in the mood to write them or not, they get written.

Morning Pages were widely used by Julia Cameron, who prescribes them to blocked artists in her book 'The Artists Way'. There are only three rules – that you write whatever comes into your head, that you write for three pages, and that you write every single morning. She believes that 'anyone who faithfully writes Morning Pages will be led to a connection with a source of wisdom within'.

Journaling can also be useful if you use it in a more ad-hoc way, as a means of working something out for yourself, or as a place to let off steam. I'd still recommend that you give regular, habit-forming journal-writing a chance before you decide if you'll continue to use it. Your Morning Pages might become two pages every evening, or a full hour of writing first thing every Monday. Follow my three tips below to give yourself the best chance of discovering your own magic.

One: find your writing a home

Most of us live busy lives, and if we are going to introduce a new habit we need to make sure that we create a space for the habit to give it a chance of 'taking hold'. Finding a home for your new journal writing includes:

- Getting a beautiful notebook that will be a pleasure to write in, and a pen that suits you – whether this is a ball-point with purple ink or a well sharpened pencil.

- Finding the right environment to do your writing. This might be in bed after your partner has left for work, or a hidden spot at the bottom of the garden, or a window-seat. Try to find somewhere you won't be disturbed, even if you have to put a sign on the door and educate the rest of your household about your journal time.

- Finding the right time of day. This might be setting your alarm half an hour earlier, or escaping for a part of your lunch hour, or just after you come in after work. The less you vary the time, the more likely it is that the writing habit will take hold.

Two: do it every day

It's useful to write your journal every day for several reasons:

- You're more likely to form a proper habit. We're more likely to maintain regular habits (brushing your teeth) than special efforts (cleaning behind the cooker).

- It's good practice to discipline yourself to do something every day that doesn't 'have' to be done – you'll strengthen your 'getting things done' muscles. You'll need those muscles to make space for yourself.

- It's great to have a regular 'check-in' as a part of your daily routine where you can take some time to work things out.

- It can be especially useful to write your Morning Pages when you don't want to. You may be experiencing resistance to writing something that needs to be written!

It's said that you have to perform a new task about 21 times before it becomes a habit. Set yourself the challenge of writing your new journal every day in its usual 'home' for 21 days in a row. If you want to stop there, that's fine – just make it to 21. How do you feel on the 22nd day?

Three: be yourself

The whole point of journaling is that you can be exactly who you are – you're not trying to impress anyone, and you don't need to worry about boring anyone to death or annoying anyone (apart from yourself!). This is the place where you can be furiously angry at someone day after day for weeks, or you can admit to yourself that you don't really want that new job you're telling everyone you're excited about. If you're feeling guilty (or embarrassed or frustrated or ashamed etc.) about anything you're writing, make a mental note of your feelings and carry on, or write the feelings down. If you're feeling twitchy about someone finding it and discovering your secrets, invest in a notebook with a lock, or find a private hiding place to keep it during the day. Let yourself go – write nonsense, write as if you were a princess, write down your plans to take over the world. Just write!

HOW TO FIND A GOOD THERAPIST

The world breaks everyone, and afterward, some are strong at the broken places.
Ernest Hemingway

Finding a place to look at your own broken places can be easier said than done. There are many different styles of therapy out there, and many different types of therapist. What you need will depend on whether you want to 'remove' a symptom or find out more about the cause, your personality, your budget, your previous experiences and many other factors.

You can start by finding a list of local therapists at www.bacp.co.uk, along with some useful information about different kinds of therapy and what to expect. You might also want to ask selected friends or colleagues if they could recommend anyone.

It might help to arrange to meet a couple of therapists for an initial appointment before you make your decision. Therapy involves committing time, effort and energy and so it's worth getting this right.

In my experience, a good therapist:

- Will be clear about their 'boundaries' (e.g. start and finish on time, have a clear contract, give you a sense that they 'know where they are')

- Will listen to you carefully and give you the feeling that they understand most of what you're saying

- Will seem authentic

- Will give you the space to cry or feel terrible or get angry without trying to make you feel better

- Won't share their own experiences or tell you what you should do

- Won't make any judgements about your experiences or decisions

Some ideas of questions to ask a therapist when you get in touch or during your first session are:

- Where do you work?
- How much does it cost?
- How long are meetings?
- Do you charge for missed appointments/holidays?
- What is your training/experience?
- How do you feel you could help me?

The most important part of therapy is often the relationship you form with the therapist. This gives you a chance to look at what kinds of relationships you form with people and why. Don't be surprised if you have strong feelings about the relationship or about something your therapist has said or done as time goes on – it can be really useful to discuss these feelings during sessions.

Above all, trust your instincts about your therapist. Do you feel safe? Do you feel you could tell this person anything? Therapy isn't a quick fix, and is often confusing or uncomfortable. It can also be a place where you feel safe enough to say the unsayable. It will help you to make sense of where you are and where you want to be, and how you're going to get there. At its best, therapy will profoundly change the rest of your life.

CLEARING SPACE FOR CREATIVITY

Conditions for creativity are to be puzzled; to concentrate; to accept conflict and tension; to be born everyday; to feel a sense of self.
Erich Fromm

Like most people I have various responsibilities in addition to being a writer, and sometimes (OK often) it's hard to find the time to focus on my writing. Whenever I feel short of time, the writing seems to be the first thing to go. My creativity is easily squashed, easily squeezed out.

Something I've learnt over the years is how important it is to clear space for my writing. There's always a huge list of 'things to do' threatening to push it out. My writing has only survived because I've learnt to fiercely protect it.

If you also struggle with dedicating time to your creativity, whether you paint, write songs or make pots, then the following ideas might help you to look at your own techniques for clearing space and how you might be able to improve on them.

One: make a commitment
Before you go any further, I'd like you to think hard about why you want to clear space in the first place. How serious are you about your art? What does it give you? What are your goals? How much energy are you willing to invest?

If you decide that you'd rather keep your creativity as 'something I do when I have the time' then that's great – you can stop feeling guilty about not spending more time on it and get on with enjoying it.

If you decide that it is centrally important to you then now is the time to make a formal commitment to it. You might want to have some fun with this and have a formal 'marriage' ceremony – let your friends and family know how serious you are, start speaking about your creative work with pride. Honour your art, and honour the artist in yourself.

Two: feed yourself

I see my own muse as needing plenty of feeding. This is an ongoing process and it needs different types of food depending on where I am in the process. Some of this food is:

- immersing myself in other writer's work
- exploring different art forms – seeing good films, going to exhibitions...
- spending time alone with nature
- speaking with writer colleagues
- reading magazines about writing
- attending writing festivals
- writing a regular journal

Maybe you could write your own list and decide to dedicate some time each week to feeding your artist.

As you're feeding (or afterwards), little ideas will start appearing like tiny green shoots. Make sure you have a notebook handy so you can jot/sketch these ideas down and use them in your work.

Three: turn up at the page

You've decided that you're serious about this, and you've collected some interesting ideas. Now comes the important bit! Julia Cameron, who helps to unblock artists, asks us to 'turn up at the page'. It's not enough that you work 'when inspiration strikes' – you need to be able to sit down and get on with it whether you're in the mood or not.

I'd recommend that you practise this by booking time into your diary (start with ten minutes if this feels daunting) and spending this time on your art without fail. If you can't get into your painting, then read what someone else thought about painting instead. If you can't concentrate on the reading, then go for a walk and think about what you're stuck on. Practise discipline.

Four: get supported

Being an artist can be lonely, especially if your art involves you working by yourself. I've found that a support network is extremely important to keep me going. I can speak to my colleagues about bits I'm stuck on, or just have a moan about how difficult I've been finding it. Having a support network can also be an important source of feedback. Feedback helps us to sharpen our tools. Artists whose work you admire are great people to learn from.

There are many different places to look for your support network. There are often local classes or groups for writing, painting etc. The internet can be a brilliant resource. Or ask your friends if they know any artists, get in touch and ask them out for a coffee. Put time and energy into building a strong, lasting network. Ask other artists how you can help them. Accept help. And have fun!

WHERE NEXT?

Once in a while you have to take a break and visit yourself.
Audrey Giorgi

A list of a few places you might try going to if you're looking to find yourself again. Take a book, your journal, or just yourself.

- the sea
- a library
- a museum of things you wouldn't usually be interested in
- a bench where you can watch the world go by
- bridges
- travelling on trains and buses
- forests
- art galleries
- a classical concert
- the cinema on your own
- an antiques shop
- a village picked at random on a map
- a fancy dress shop
- the children's section of a bookshop
- under your duvet
- a friend's house when they're away on holiday
- under a tree
- a churchyard
- your back doorstep
- wherever you are RIGHT NOW

FURTHER READING

It makes me laugh when I go to a bookstore and see all those titles about controlling your life. You're lucky if you can control your bladder.
Rita Mae Brown

These books haven't helped me to control my life (or my bladder) but they have all helped me with my own questions, and left me a slightly different person than I was before.

General musing
These books might help you with your own questions.

Astley, Neil (Ed.). *Staying Alive: Real Poems for Unreal Times*, Bloodaxe Books, 2002. If you don't already have this and at least thirty more books of poetry in your bookshelves, go out and buy it immediately. Be warned... you may become addicted...

Bly, Robert, Booth, William (Ed.). *A Little Book on the Human Shadow*, HarperCollins, 1992. The poet speaks about how we chuck everything we don't like about ourselves into a bag we drag behind us, and how we can start 'swallowing' these parts of us again.

Bronson, Po. *What Should I Do With My Life?* Vintage, 2004. The ultimate career guide for those of us who love questions.

Cameron, Julie. *The Artists Way,* Jeremy P Tarcher, 2002. A cult book on how to unblock your creativity – if you get one book on creativity, get this one.

Carver, Raymond. *Where I'm Calling From: Selected Stories*, The Harvill Press, 1995. My all-time favourite author – so ordinary and wise.

Chodron, Pema. *When Things Fall Apart: Heart Advice for Difficult Times*, Element Books, 2005. Pema speaks a lot about moving towards what is difficult. Good stuff in a lot of her books.

Fromm, Erich. *To Have or To Be?* Continuum Publishing Group, 2005. Good question.

Goldberg, Natalie. *Writing Down The Bones*, Shambhala Publications, 1986. Guaranteed to start words flowing from your pen.

Lammot, Anne. *Bird by Bird: Some instructions on Writing and Life*, Anchor Books, 1995. This woman is seriously funny and also has a lot of very sensible things to say about getting the work done. She invented 'shitty first drafts' which are a very useful thing to do.

Lane, John. *Timeless Simplicity*, Green Books, 2001. A beautiful little book on paring back and on appreciating what we have.

Moore, Lorrie. *Birds of America*, Faber and Faber, 1999. A wonderful novelist – she hits the nail on the head and it hurts.

Oliver, Mary. *Wild Geese*, Bloodaxe Books, 2004. Luminous, spiritual poetry about nature and the meaning of it all.

Sarton, May. *A House By The Sea: A Journal*, W. W. Norton, 1996. Sarton's journals are all wonderful – this describes her first happy year in a new house.

Suzuki, Shunryu. *Zen Mind, Beginner's Mind*. Weatherhill Inc, 1973. I certainly don't understand all of this but it makes me want to keep trying.

Ueland, Brenda. *If You Want To Write*, Greywolf Press, 1938. A classic, full of fizzing passion and wise words. I would have loved to have had Brenda living down the road so I could pop in for cups of tea.

Specific topics

The following books are about specific issues that may be blocking you.

Beattie, Melody. *Codependent No More: How to Stop Controlling Others and Start Caring for Yourself*, Hazelden Information & Educational Services, 1989. Does what it says on the tin.

Forster, Mark. *Get Everything Done and Still Have Time to Play*, Help Yourself, 2000. If you're hopeless at time management, this is a good little book with some advice I've held onto and still use.

Lerner, Harriet. *The Dance of Intimacy: A Woman's Guide to Courageous Acts of Change in Key Relationships*, HarperPerennial, 2003. If you suspect you may find intimacy difficulty.

Nemeth, Maria. *The Energy of Money*, Wellspring/Ballantine, 2000. A very good book to help you start teasing out the complications of your relationship with money.

Orbach, Susie. *On Eating*, Penguin Books, 2002. For anyone who struggles with food.

Rogers, Carl R. *Becoming Partners: Marriage and its alternatives*, Constable and Company, 1973. Food for thought on how we might make good partnerships.

Rowe, Dorothy. *Depression: The Way Out of Your Prison*, Brunner-Routledge, 2003. A well-known writer on depression.

Weekes, Claire. *Self-help for your nerves*, HarperCollins, 2000. For anyone whose anxiety is getting the better of them. Now go out and find your own favourite books!